THE NOW THAT'S WHAT I CALL MUSIC BOOK

Pete Selby and Andy Healing

SIMON & SCHUSTER

London · New York · Sydney · Toronto · New Delhi

A CBS COMPANY

Welcome

This book is for you if you've ever fallen in love with pop music.

You may have bought your first single in the mid-eighties, in thrall to The Thompson Twins or dazzled by Duran Duran. Maybe Erasure earned your adoration, perhaps Pet Shop Boys piqued your interest. If a little younger, your introduction to a life spent listening to music might have been Minogue, Michael or McFly; Beautiful South, Britney or Black Eyed Peas; Robbie, Ronan or Rihanna.

Throughout the last three decades NOW That's What I Call Music has been chronicling the changing patterns of pop. Three times a year, a new set of music-mad minions joins the ranks of those who can fondly remember their first NOW.

This book conjures memories but also brings you right up to the present day. It takes you from 1983 to 2015, divulging some lesser-known facts about many of the featured artists along the way. For each edition, it unearths links between performers and songs; notes where popstars were in such good form that they managed a 'Double Feature', appearing twice on one album; and pays tribute to those joining or leaving the NOW story. There's also a set of infographics that highlight the numbers behind the tracklistings.

It's a history of the pop world as captured by NOW That's What I Call Music. It's the soundtrack to your life, and we hope you enjoy it.

Contents

A BRIEF HISTORY OF *NOW*

The idea of assembling singles by different artists on to compilations was not a new concept in the early '80s. Record shop patrons were used to seeing single-label primers like the Motown Chartbusters series on their racks alongside specialist companies like K-Tel and Ronco, who were well versed in using TV ad campaigns to tempt potential customers.

The Virgin record label was enjoying a particularly successful year in 1983 and the idea was hatched to put together an album showcasing the biggest hit singles from the finest artists on their roster. The brainchild of record execs Stephen Navin and Jon Webster, the concept was routed via Virgin Head of A&R, Simon Draper, to his cousin Richard Branson, the founder of the label. Meanwhile, at rival record company EMI, Managing Director Peter Jamieson was putting together a similar plot and over time, the idea of a joint venture was mooted and agreed. Able to call upon popular tracks from the two labels, the nascent *NOW* would prove to be a compelling proposition.

You may be curious as to how the series first got its distinctive name. The story goes that while browsing a bric-a-brac shop one day, Branson was struck by a '20s poster ad extolling the virtues of Danish bacon by, curiously, featuring a pig listening to a singing chicken. The strapline for the ad? 'Now That's What I Call Music'. The poster was purchased and installed in the Virgin office, where it would catch the attention when names for the first album were being bandied around. Distinctive, memorable, authentic. *NOW* that's what I call music!

The album was an instant success over Christmas 1983 and led to follow-up editions, establishing the series which is still running today, over thirty years later. *NOW* not only releases three numbered editions per year (at Easter, in the summer and in time for Christmas) but also releases genre-based spin-offs.

So much has changed in the world over the last three decades, including the way we purchase and listen to music, but *NOW* remains

Now. That's what I call Music

stronger than ever. Richard Branson is clear about why the series continues to endure:

'It's true that the market has been transformed from the one that Virgin Records first operated in; however, the reasons that people decide to purchase a *NOW* record remain the same. Each year there is a collection of songs which everyone in the country becomes familiar with: they'll be played on the radio, at parties, on nights out, in the office and at festivals. Those songs will represent a whole host of emotions and memories for people, so as well as a collection of great songs; it's those memories which people get when they listen to a *NOW* album. Whether you buy vinyl or stream, it doesn't change a thing in that sense.'

So, here it is. Ninety-one albums that trace the story of *NOW* over thirty-two glorious years. Over to you, Phil Collins...

Double Album
30 GREAT TRACKS
including 11 Number Ones

Madness · Culture Club · Kajagoogoo · Duran Duran
UB40 · Phil Collins · Paul Young · Tracey Ullman · Limahl · Genesis
Rod Stewart · Howard Jones · Simple Minds · The Cure · and many more . . .

NOW
That's What I Call Music

RELEASED 28 NOVEMBER 1983

DOUBLE FEATURE
UB40
CULTURE CLUB
KAJAGOOGOO

▶ Birmingham-based reggae veterans **UB40**, 80s pop behemoths **Culture Club** and Leighton Buzzard synth poppers **Kajagoogoo** all featured twice on this introductory *NOW*. Our old friends **UB40** appear more times across the first ten volumes than any other artist – seven in total.

TRACKLISTING NOW 1

Record 1 Side 1

1 You Can't Hurry Love **Phil Collins**
2 Is There Something I Should Know **Duran Duran**
3 Red Red Wine **UB40**
4 Only For Love **Limahl**
5 Temptation **Heaven 17**
6 Give It Up **KC and the Sunshine Band**
7 Double Dutch **Malcolm McLaren**
8 Total Eclipse Of The Heart **Bonnie Tyler**

Record 1 Side 2

1 Karma Chameleon **Culture Club**
2 The Safety Dance **Men Without Hats**
3 Too Shy **Kajagoogoo**
4 Moonlight Shadow **Mike Oldfield**
5 Down Under **Men At Work**
6 (Hey You) The Rock Steady Crew **Rock Steady Crew**
7 Baby Jane **Rod Stewart**
8 Wherever I Lay My Hat (That's My Home) **Paul Young**

Record 2 Side 1

1 Candy Girl **New Edition**
2 Big Apple **Kajagoogoo**
3 Let's Stay Together **Tina Turner**
4 (Keep Feeling) Fascination **The Human League**
5 New Song **Howard Jones**
6 Please Don't Make Me Cry **UB40**
7 Tonight, I Celebrate My Love **Peabo Bryson & Roberta Flack**

Record 2 Side 2

1 They Don't Know **Tracey Ullman**
2 Kissing With Confidence **Will Powers**
3 That's All **Genesis**
4 The Lovecats **The Cure**
5 Waterfront **Simple Minds**
6 The Sun And The Rain **Madness**
7 Victims **Culture Club**

▶ Sales of **Mike Oldfield**'s *Tubular Bells* album helped Richard Branson's Virgin record label grow throughout the '70s and early '80s, so it was appropriate that he featured on the very first *NOW*, which was released as a partnership between the Virgin and EMI labels.

▶ 'Kissing With Confidence' was the only hit **Will Powers** managed in the UK, but there's no shortage of familiar names in the background: the song was co-written by **Steve Winwood** ('Higher Love', *NOW 8*), **CHIC**'s **Nile Rodgers** ('Sensitivity', *NOW 64*) and maverick performer-producer Todd Rundgren (no *NOW* appearances to date). Vocals were contributed by an uncredited Carly Simon, famous for 'You're So Vain' and other hits.

NOW
That's what I call
music
II

DOUBLE ALBUM
30 Top Chart Hits
by original artists

Culture Club · Nena · Frankie Goes To Hollywood ·
David Bowie · Queen · Tracey Ullman · Thompson Twins ·
Eurythmics · Paul McCartney · Howard Jones · and many more…

RELEASED 26 MARCH 1984

HELLO
QUEEN

GOODBYE
THE SMITHS

▶ Pop polymath **Thomas Dolby** has links with other *NOW 2* artists. He played live with **David Bowie** at Live Aid and with **Howard Jones** at the 1985 Grammys. He also played keyboard on the **Thompson Twins** pre-fame album *Set*.

Record 1 Side 1

1. Radio Ga Ga **Queen**
2. Wouldn't It Be Good **Nik Kershaw**
3. Hold Me Now **Thompson Twins**
4. Get Out Of Your Lazy Bed **Matt Bianco**
5. More, More, More **Carmel**
6. Michael Caine **Madness**
7. Only You **The Flying Pickets**

Record 1 Side 2

1. 99 Red Balloons **Nena**
2. Girls Just Wanna Have Fun **Cyndi Lauper**
3. My Guy **Tracey Ullman**
4. Breakin' Down (Sugar Samba) **Julia & Company**
5. Break My Stride **Matthew Wilder**
6. That's Livin' Alright **Joe Fagin**
7. I Gave You My Heart (Didn't I) **Hot Chocolate**
8. Bird Of Paradise **Snowy White**

Record 2 Side 1

1. Relax **Frankie Goes to Hollywood**
2. Here Comes The Rain Again **Eurythmics**
3. What Is Love? **Howard Jones**
4. What Difference Does It Make **The Smiths**
5. (Feels Like) Heaven **Fiction Factory**
6. The Politics Of Dancing **Re-Flex**
7. Hyperactive! **Thomas Dolby**
8. Wishful Thinking **China Crisis**

Record 2 Side 2

1. Modern Love **David Bowie**
2. It's A Miracle **Culture Club**
3. Undercover Of The Night **The Rolling Stones**
4. Wonderland **Big Country**
5. Run Runaway **Slade**
6. New Moon On Monday **Duran Duran**
7. Pipes Of Peace **Paul McCartney**

▶ Ipswich Wide Boy **Nik Kershaw** spent more weeks in the UK Top 40 in 1984 than any other artist. His appearance here marks the first of his four *NOW* entries – all within the first six volumes. However, his most successful songwriting credit – 'The One and Only' by Chesney Hawkes – has never appeared on a *NOW*.

▶ Nutty funsters **Madness** spent more weeks on the singles chart during the '80s than any other group. They would rack up seven *NOW* entries in total, however, singer Cathal Smyth, aka Chas Smash, also wrote 'Listen To Your Father' for **Feargal Sharkey** on *NOW 4*.

DOUBLE ALBUM   30 TOP THIRTY HITS   ORIGINAL ARTISTS

NOW 3
THAT'S WHAT I CALL *music*

DURAN DURAN
QUEEN •• BRONSKI BEAT
NIK KERSHAW •• CYNDI LAUPER
PHIL COLLINS •• STYLE COUNCIL
TINA TURNER •• ULTRAVOX
HOWARD JONES •• DAVID SYLVIAN
ALISON MOYET •• **WHAM!**
ORCHESTRAL MANOEUVRES IN THE DARK
BOB MARLEY AND THE WAILERS
GRANDMASTER AND MELLE MEL
FRANKIE GOES TO HOLLYWOOD
THOMPSON TWINS

RELEASED 23 JULY 1984

HELLO
BANANARAMA
GOODBYE
BLANCMANGE

▶ It may have been raining men for **The Weather Girls** on their only credited *NOW* showing, but the ensuing years haven't been a desert for their singer Martha Wash – with **Todd Terry** in tow, she would be back with 'Keep On Jumpin'' on *NOW 34* and 'Something Goin' On' on *NOW 37*. Uncredited, she would also appear on **C+C Music Factory**'s 'Gonna Make You Sweat' (*NOW 19*).

TRACKLISTING NOW 3

Record 1 Side 1

1 The Reflex Duran Duran
2 I Won't Let The Sun Go Down On Me
   Nik Kershaw
3 Thinking Of You Sister Sledge
4 Locomotion Orchestral Manoeuvres
   in the Dark
5 Dancing With Tears In My Eyes
   Ultravox
6 Pearl In The Shell Howard Jones
7 Don't Tell Me Blancmange
8 Against All Odds (Take A Look
   At Me Now) Phil Collins

Record 1 Side 2

1 Two Tribes Frankie Goes to
   Hollywood
2 White Lines (Don't Don't Do It)
   Grandmaster Flash & The Furious Five
3 Nelson Mandela The Special AKA
4 Love Wars Womack & Womack
5 You're The Best Thing
   The Style Council
6 One Love/People Get Ready
   Bob Marley & The Wailers
7 Smalltown Boy Bronski Beat

Record 2 Side 1

1 I Want To Break Free Queen
2 Time After Time Cyndi Lauper
3 Love Resurrection Alison Moyet
4 Young At Heart The Bluebells
5 Robert De Niro's Waiting
   Bananarama
6 Dr Mabuse Propaganda
7 What's Love Got To Do With It
   Tina Turner
8 When You're Young And In Love
   The Flying Pickets

Record 2 Side 2

1 Wake Me Up Before You Go-Go
   Wham!
2 You Take Me Up Thompson Twins
3 It's Raining Men
   The Weather Girls
4 Dance Me Up Gary Glitter
5 Susanna The Art Company
6 One Better Day Madness
7 Red Guitar David Sylvian

▶ In the '80s, songs about nuclear war were frequently hits. **Ultravox**'s 'Dancing With Tears In My Eyes' is an example from this *NOW,* with others including **Nena**'s '99 Red Balloons' (*NOW 2*), 'The War Song' by **Culture Club** (*NOW 4*), 'Land Of Confusion' by **Genesis** (*NOW 9*) and **Morrissey**'s 'Everyday Is Like Sunday' (*NOW 12*), with 'Too Young To Die' by **Jamiroquai** (*NOW 26*) and 'Four Minute Warning' by **Mark Owen** (*NOW 56*) taking up the issue a little later.

▶ **The Art Company** were the first Dutch group to appear on a *NOW* album but by no means the last – as our story progresses, we will also encounter **2 Unlimited** (eight *NOW* appearances from volumes *20* to *30*) and **Vengaboys** (six consecutive inclusions from *NOW 41* to *46*). **Mai Tai** await us on *NOW 5*.

DOUBLE ALBUM·32 CHART-HOGGIN' HITS·ORIGINAL ARTISTS.

UB 40
JOHN WAITE
BIG COUNTRY
PAUL McCARTNEY
ELTON JOHN
STATUS QUO

KIM WILDE
CULTURE CLUB
GIORGIO MORODER WITH PHILIP OAKEY
NIK KERSHAW · POINTER SISTERS
WILD EXPRESS ORAT
RAY PARKER JR.

BRONSKI BEAT
FEARGAL SHARKEY
EUGENE WILDE
EURYTHMICS
TINA TURNER
QUEEN
O.M.D.

NOW
THAT'S WHAT I CALL
music **4**

MALCOLM McLAREN
THE KANE GANG
LIMAHL
LIONEL RICHIE
THOMPSON TWINS
· NICK HEYWARD

HEAVEN 17
ROCKWELL
U2

RELEASED 26 NOVEMBER 1984

HELLO
STATUS QUO
GOODBYE
THOMPSON TWINS

▶ The first of six *NOW* entries for the Isle of Wight's favourite jazz pop funkateers, **Level 42** – one each year spanning 1984–89. On his record company's instruction, Mark King (the guy who put the 'slap' in slap bass) insured his thumb for the princely sum of £3 million, making it the most valuable digit in pop, by our reckoning.

TRACKLISTING NOW 4

Record 1 Side 1

1 No More Lonely Nights
Paul McCartney
2 Together In Electric Dreams
Philip Oakey & Giorgio Moroder
3 Why? **Bronski Beat**
4 The Neverending Story **Limahl**
5 Warning Sign **Nick Heyward**
6 Missing You **John Waite**
7 Farewell My Summer Love
Michael Jackson
8 Hello **Lionel Richie**

Record 1 Side 2

1 The War Song **Culture Club**
2 Passengers **Elton John**
3 Too Late For Goodbyes **Julian Lennon**
4 Shout To The Top **The Style Council**
5 Doctor! Doctor! **Thompson Twins**
6 Sunset Now **Heaven 17**
7 Respect Yourself **The Kane Gang**
8 Private Dancer **Tina Turner**

Record 2 Side 1

1 It's A Hard Life **Queen**
2 The Wanderer **Status Quo**
3 East Of Eden **Big Country**
4 Pride (In The Name Of Love) **U2**
5 Listen To Your Father **Feargal Sharkey**
6 Tesla Girls **Orchestral Manoeuvres in the Dark**
7 The Second Time **Kim Wilde**
8 Human Racing **Nik Kershaw**

Record 2 Side 2

1 Ghostbusters **Ray Parker Jr**
2 If It Happens Again **UB40**
3 Jump (For My Love) **The Pointer Sisters**
4 Hot Water **Level 42**
5 Sexcrime (Nineteen Eighty-Four) **Eurythmics**
6 Somebody's Watching Me **Rockwell**
7 Madam Butterfly (Un Bel Di Vedremo) **Malcolm McLaren**
8 Gotta Get You Home Tonight **Eugene Wilde**

▶ **Julian Lennon** would land two entries in the *NOW* canon before his famous father made his own *NOW* debut with a re-released 'Imagine' on *NOW 45*. The video for 'Too Late For Goodbyes' marked the final – and most unlikely – directorial role for notorious US filmmaker Sam Peckinpah.

▶ So with more than 170 million record sales to their name, it's a big *NOW* hello to Dublin's **U2**. 'Pride' is their first of nineteen *NOW* entries spanning the next twenty-five years and ranks them third as 'Group With Most Appearances'. It will be a while before we meet the acts at No.1 and No.2.

THIRTY TOP 30 HITS– DOUBLE ALBUM

NOW
THAT'S WHAT I CALL
music **5**

KOOL and the GANG
U2
THE POWER STATION
Harold Faltermeyer
CHINA CRISIS
Phil Collins
MADNESS
MAI·TAI
DURAN·DURAN
SISTER SLEDGE
SCRITTI POLITTI
BRYAN FERRY
Stephen tintin duffy
Simply Red
CONWAY BROS
Howard Jones
STYLE·COUNCIL
DAVID BOWIE
MARILLION
SIMPLE MINDS
THE DAMNED
FINE YOUNG CANNIBALS

RELEASED 5 AUGUST 1985

**HELLO
SIMPLY RED**

**GOODBYE
HOWARD JONES**

▶ Serving as the theme tune to the 1985 film *The Breakfast Club*, 'Don't You (Forget About Me)' appeared here as recorded by eight-time *NOW* contributors **Simple Minds** – but they weren't the first act to be offered the song. Fellow *NOW 5* star **Bryan Ferry** turned down the opportunity to record it, as did *NOW 10* and *11* contributor **Billy Idol**.

TRACKLISTING NOW 5

Record 1 Side 1

1 A View To A Kill **Duran Duran**
2 The Word Girl **Scritti Politti**
3 Axel F **Harold Faltermeyer**
4 Johnny Come Home
   Fine Young Cannibals
5 In Too Deep **Dead Or Alive**
6 Icing On The Cake **Stephen**
   'Tin Tin' Duffy
7 Cherish **Kool & The Gang**
8 Every Time You Go Away **Paul Young**

Record 1 Side 2

1 Kayleigh **Marillion**
2 Slave To Love **Bryan Ferry**
3 This Is Not America **David Bowie &**
   The Pat Metheny Group
4 Don't You (Forget About Me)
   Simple Minds
5 Get It On (Bang A Gong)
   The Power Station
6 Black Man Ray **China Crisis**
7 One More Night **Phil Collins**

Record 2 Side 1

1 Frankie **Sister Sledge**
2 History **Mai Tai**
3 Money's Too Tight (To Mention)
   Simply Red
4 Feel So Real **Steve Arrington**
5 Round And Around **Jaki Graham**
6 Turn It Up **The Conway Brothers**
7 Magic Touch **Loose Ends**
8 N-N-Nineteen Not Out
   The Commentators

Record 2 Side 2

1 The Unforgettable Fire **U2**
2 Walls Come Tumbling Down
   The Style Council
3 Walking On Sunshine
   Katrina and The Waves
4 Out In The Fields **Gary Moore**
   and Phil Lynott
5 The Shadow Of Love **The Damned**
6 Life In One Day **Howard Jones**
7 Love Don't Live Here Anymore
   Jimmy Nail

▶ The holy triumvirate of glam-rock superstars were out in force on *NOW 5* – **David Bowie** and Roxy Music's **Bryan Ferry** appeared in their own right, while Marc Bolan was represented via **The Power Station**'s 'Get It On (Bang A Gong)'. **The Power Station**'s **Robert Palmer** would next appear on *NOW 8* with a cover version of the Jimmy Jam and Terry Lewis song, 'I Didn't Mean To Turn You On'. Jam and Lewis, incidentally, also helm tracks from both **Janet Jackson** and **The Human League** on the same volume.

▶ Geordie thespian **Jimmy Nail** made the first of four *NOW* appearances here with 'Love Don't Live Here Anymore', the song originally a hit for US soul band **Rose Royce**, who would later feature on *NOW 12* with 'Car Wash'. Madonna also recorded the song on her 1984 album *Like A Virgin*.

NOW
THAT'S WHAT I CALL
music 6

· QUEEN · FEARGAL SHARKEY · PHIL COLLINS & MARILYN MARTIN · ELTON JOHN · LEVEL 42 · ARCADIA ·
· EURYTHMICS · UB4O · MADNESS · NIK KERSHAW · SIMPLE MINDS · MIDGE URE · MARILLION · TINA TURNER · KATE BUSH ·
PLUS MANY MORE

RELEASED 25 NOVEMBER 1985

HELLO
THE COMMUNARDS
GOODBYE
NIK KERSHAW

▶ **Phil Collins** saw four of his first seven *NOW* entries taken from a film soundtrack. 'Separate Lives' is lifted from *White Nights* (*NOW 6*), 'Against All Odds' (*NOW 3*) from the Taylor Hackford film of the same name, and both 'A Groovy Kind Of Love' (*NOW 13*) and 'Two Hearts' (*NOW 14*) from knockabout Great Train Robbery caper *Buster*.

Record 1 Side 1

1 *One Vision* Queen
2 *When A Heart Beats* Nik Kershaw
3 *A Good Heart* Feargal Sharkey
4 *There Must Be An Angel (Playing With My Heart)* Eurythmics
5 *Alive And Kicking* Simple Minds
6 *It's Only Love (Live)* Tina Turner with Bryan Adams
7 *Empty Rooms* Gary Moore
8 *Lavender* Marillion

Record 1 Side 2

1 *Nikita* Elton John
2 *Running Up That Hill (A Deal With God)* Kate Bush
3 *Something About You* Level 42
4 *We Don't Need Another Hero (Thunderdome)* Tina Turner
5 *Don't Break My Heart* UB40
6 *Separate Lives* Phil Collins & Marilyn Martin
7 *She's So Beautiful* Cliff Richard

Record 2 Side 1

1 *Election Day* Arcadia
2 *I Got You Babe* UB40 Feat. Chrissie Hynde
3 *Blue* Fine Young Cannibals
4 *If I Was* Midge Ure
5 *Cities In Dust* Siouxsie & The Banshees
6 *Uncle Sam* Madness
7 *Lost Weekend* Lloyd Cole & The Commotions
8 *You Are My World* The Communards

Record 2 Side 2

1 *Just For Money* Paul Hardcastle
2 *Miami Vice Theme* Jan Hammer
3 *Body Rock* Maria Vidal
4 *Tarzan Boy* Baltimora
5 *Body And Soul* Mai Tai
6 *Single Life* Cameo
7 *Mated* David Grant & Jaki Graham

▶ **Cliff Richard**'s 'She's So Beautiful' from Dave Clark's *Time* musical marked the first *NOW* entry for the pop legend. The track was recorded with **Stevie Wonder**, who also appeared in collaborative form with **Eurythmics**, honking his harmonica all over 'There Must Be An Angel (Playing With My Heart)' on *NOW 6*. The former Stevland Judkins has never appeared on *NOW* as a credited artist in his own right.

▶ 'Election Day' adds to an overall tally of eight **Duran Duran**-related appearances across the first eight volumes – six from the band and two from their side projects: **Arcadia**, featured here, and **The Power Station**, who appear on *NOW 5*. **Grace Jones**, who makes an uncredited cameo on 'Election Day', would feature only once as a solo artist, on *NOW 8*, with 'I'm Not Perfect (But I'm Perfect For You)'.

MOST FEATURED ARTISTS

CREDITED APPEARANCES ONLY

29 ROBBIE WILLIAMS

26 RIHANNA

23 KYLIE MINOGUE

21 GIRLS ALOUD

20 CALVIN HARRIS

20 DAVID GUETTA

19 BRITNEY SPEARS

19 SUGABABES

19 U2

16 KATY PERRY

Rihanna

THE TOP 5 BESTSELLING *NOWs*

2 million				
NOW 44	**NOW 50**	**NOW 47**	**NOW 29**	**NOW 41**
Christmas release	Christmas release	Christmas release	Christmas release	Christmas release
10 No.1 Singles	8 No.1 Singles	10 No.1 Singles	3 No.1 Singles	8 No.1 Singles

1.5 million

1 million

0.5 million

0

THOSE *NOW 1* COVER STARS. HOW DID THEY DO?

Madness · Culture Club · Kajagoogoo · Duran Duran
UB40 · Phil Collins · Paul Young · Tracey Ullman · Limahl · Genesis
Rod Stewart · Howard Jones · Simple Minds · The Cure · and many more . . .

NOW

That's What I Call Music

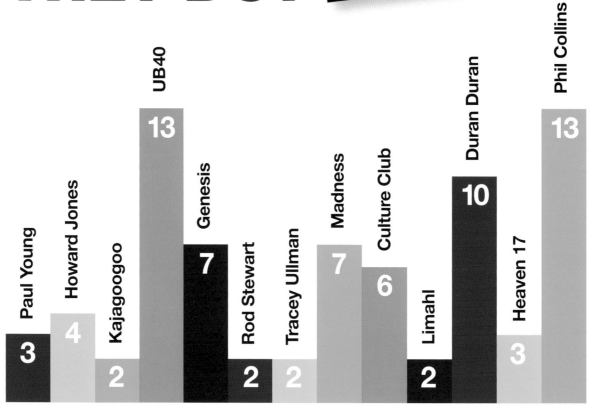

Paul Young	Howard Jones	Kajagoogoo	UB40	Genesis	Rod Stewart	Tracey Ullman	Madness	Culture Club	Limahl	Duran Duran	Heaven 17	Phil Collins
3	4	2	13	7	2	2	7	6	2	10	3	13

Total *NOW* appearances since 1983

29
TOTAL SOLO
APPEARANCES

28
TOP 10 SOLO
SINGLES ON *NOW*

6
APPEARANCES
WITH
TAKE THAT

17
BRIT
AWARDS

Hats off to the artist with the most *NOW* appearances of all time

ROBBIE WILLIAMS

8
NO.1 SOLO
SINGLES
ON *NOW*

11
NO.1 ALBUMS
IN THE UK

77
MILLION
GLOBAL
RECORD
SALES

32 TOP CHART HITS

NOW
THAT'S WHAT I CALL
music **7**

QUEEN
BONUS TRACK
NOW 7
A KIND OF MAGIC

PETER GABRIEL · WHAM! · DAVID BOWIE · GENESIS · THE HOUSEMARTINS · DOCTOR AND THE MEDICS · PET SHOP BOYS · LEVEL 42
SIMPLE MINDS · UB40 · A-HA · SLY FOX · OWEN PAUL · CHRIS DE BURGH · PATTI LA BELLE & MICHAEL McDONALD · SIMPLY RED · BILLY OCEAN
PLUS MANY MORE

RELEASED 11 AUGUST 1986

HELLO
THE HOUSEMARTINS

GOODBYE
DAVID BOWIE

▶ The **Pet Shop Boys** *NOW* odyssey began here and to date takes in eleven appearances as named artists. Lead singer Neil Tennant was a music journalist before hitting the charts – an opposite journey to that made by **Furniture** main-man Jim Irvin, now a writer for the music magazine *Mojo* when he's not co-writing hits like 'The Weekend' (**Michael Gray**, *NOW 59*).

Record 1 Side 1

1 *Sledgehammer* Peter Gabriel
2 *Sing Our Own Song* UB40
3 *Let's Go All The Way* Sly Fox
4 *Lessons In Love* Level 42
5 *Opportunities (Let's Make Lots Of Money)* Pet Shop Boys
6 *Sinful!* Pete Wylie
7 *Camouflage* Stan Ridgway
8 *Paranoimia* Art of Noise with Max Headroom

Record 1 Side 2

1 *The Lady In Red* Chris De Burgh
2 *Absolute Beginners* David Bowie
3 *Invisible Touch* Genesis
4 *All The Things She Said* Simple Minds
5 *Happy Hour* The Housemartins
6 *Look Away* Big Country
7 *Brilliant Mind* Furniture
8 *Call Of The Wild* Midge Ure

Record 2 Side 1

1 *The Edge Of Heaven* Wham!
2 *My Favourite Waste Of Time* Owen Paul
3 *Too Good To Be Forgotten* Amazulu
4 *Spirit In The Sky* Doctor & The Medics
5 *Venus* Bananarama
6 *New Beginning (Mamba Seyra)* Bucks Fizz
7 *Hunting High And Low* a-ha
8 *Holding Back The Years* Simply Red
9 *A Kind Of Magic* Queen

Record 2 Side 2

1 *When The Going Gets Tough, The Tough Get Going* Billy Ocean
2 *Set Me Free* Jaki Graham
3 *I Can't Wait* Nu Shooz
4 *Amityville (The House On The Hill)* Lovebug Starski
5 *Headlines* Midnight Star
6 *You And Me Tonight* Aurra
7 *On My Own* Patti Labelle and Michael McDonald
8 *Bang Zoom (Let's Go Go)* The Real Roxanne with Hitman Howie Tee

▶ By some distance, the most successful Norwegian artists in the UK charts, three-time *NOW* contributors *a-ha* hold the world record for the largest attendance at a paid-for concert, attracting 198,000 punters to a 1991 gig at the Maracanã Stadium, Rio De Janeiro, Brazil. Their most recent *NOW* connection was 'Take On Me' being sampled by **Pitbull feat. Christina Aguilera** on *NOW 85*.

▶ **Billy Ocean** co-penned 'When The Going Gets Tough, The Tough Get Going' with writer-producer 'Mutt' Lange and would see the song appear again on *NOW 42*, this time recorded by **Boyzone**. Lange's other *NOW* contributions include 'The Only Thing That Looks Good On Me Is You' (**Bryan Adams**, *NOW 34*), four singles with then-wife **Shania Twain** (*NOW 39* and *44* to *46*), and 'Don't Let Me Be The Last To Know' (**Britney Spears**, *NOW 49*).

DURAN DURAN · PET SHOP BOYS · COMMUNARDS · GENESIS · CAMEO · GRACE JONES · JERMAINE STEWART · PETER GABRIEL/KATE BUSH
HUMAN LEAGUE · THE HOUSEMARTINS · MADNESS · STATUS QUO · HUEY LEWIS AND THE NEWS · KIM WILDE
PLUS MANY MORE.

RELEASED 24 NOVEMBER 1986

**HELLO
JANET JACKSON**

**GOODBYE
JAKI GRAHAM**

▶ *NOW 8* marks the only (albeit uncredited) appearance by American rockers **Aerosmith** on **Run DMC**'s cover of 'Walk This Way'. It would be another twelve years before we saw the return of the Hollis hip-hop trio, with their 'It's Like That' (*NOW 39*) keeping **Spice Girls**' 'Stop' off the top spot and denying the girls a run of ten No.1s from their first ten singles. That's the way it is.

Record 1 Side 1

1 *Notorious* Duran Duran
2 *Suburbia* Pet Shop Boys
3 *Walk This Way* Run DMC
4 *Don't Leave Me This Way* The Communards
5 *Breakout* Swing Out Sister
6 *Higher Love* Steve Winwood
7 *(Forever) Live And Die* Orchestral Manoeuvres in the Dark
8 *In Too Deep* Genesis

Record 1 Side 2

1 *Word Up* Cameo
2 *I'm Not Perfect (But I'm Perfect For You)* Grace Jones
3 *Showing Out (Get Fresh At The Weekend)* Mel & Kim
4 *We Don't Have To Take Our Clothes Off* Jermaine Stewart
5 *Step Right Up* Jaki Graham
6 *What Have You Done For Me Lately* Janet Jackson
7 *Human* The Human League
8 *I Want To Wake Up With You* Boris Gardiner

Record 2 Side 1

1 *Don't Give Up* Peter Gabriel and Kate Bush
2 *Think For A Minute* The Housemartins
3 *(Waiting For) The Ghost-Train* Madness
4 *In The Army Now* Status Quo
5 *Stuck With You* Huey Lewis & The News
6 *One Great Thing* Big Country
7 *Greetings To The New Brunette* Billy Bragg
8 *(I Just) Died In Your Arms* Cutting Crew

Record 2 Side 2

1 *You Keep Me Hanging On* Kim Wilde
2 *Calling All The Heroes* It Bites
3 *Waterloo* Doctor & The Medics
4 *French Kissin' In The USA* Debbie Harry
5 *I Didn't Mean To Turn You On* Robert Palmer
6 *The Wizard* Paul Hardcastle
7 *(They Long To Be) Close To You* Gwen Guthrie
8 *Every Loser Wins* Nick Berry

▶ **Nick Berry**'s 'Every Loser Wins' was the third of three *EastEnders* related Top 20 singles in 1986 but the only one to be canonised by *NOW*, thus disappointing Anita Dobson, Letitia Dean and Paul Medford. Originally sung by his character in the show – cheeky pot-boy Wicksy – Berry would land the second biggest-selling UK single of 1986, beaten only by **The Communards**, also included here. Both would return.

▶ While he has no solo artist credits to his name, globe-straddling disco behemoth **Nile Rodgers** has his hand in three separate tracks on *NOW 8* – **Duran Duran**'s 'Notorious', **Grace Jones**'s 'I'm Not Perfect (But I'm Perfect For You)' and **Steve Winwood**'s 'Higher Love'. **The Chic Organisation**'s majordomo is either playing guitar, producing or both. He'd be back much later assisting **Daft Punk** on *NOW 85*'s 'Get Lucky'. Good times!

NOW 9

THAT'S WHAT I CALL
music

BEN E. KING · BOY GEORGE · CURIOSITY KILLED THE CAT · SIMPLY RED · A-HA · FREDDIE MERCURY
5 STAR · MENTAL AS ANYTHING · GENESIS · UB40 · BON JOVI · WESTWORLD · JACKIE WILSON
PLUS MANY MORE

RELEASED 23 MARCH 1987

**HELLO
ERASURE
GOODBYE
GARY MOORE**

▶ **Pepsi & Shirlie** first found fame as backing singers for **Wham!** and can be heard on 'Wake Me Up Before You Go-Go' (*NOW 3*) and 'The Edge Of Heaven' (*NOW 7*). A little bit later, the duo reunited to contribute backing vocals to **Geri Halliwell**'s 'Bag It Up' (*NOW 45*).

Record 1 Side 1

1 *Reet Petite* **Jackie Wilson**
2 *Live It Up* **Mental As Anything**
3 *The Right Thing* **Simply Red**
4 *Sometimes* **Erasure**
5 *C'est La Vie* **Robbie Nevil**
6 *You Sexy Thing* **Hot Chocolate**
7 *It Doesn't Have To Be This Way* **The Blow Monkeys**
8 *Caravan Of Love* **The Housemartins**

Record 1 Side 2

1 *Everything I Own* **Boy George**
2 *Rat In Mi Kitchen* **UB40**
3 *Big Fun* **The Gap Band**
4 *Stay Out Of My Life* **Five Star**
5 *Heartache* **Pepsi & Shirlie**
6 *Trick Of The Night* **Bananarama**
7 *Take My Breath Away* **Berlin**

Record 2 Side 1

1 *The Great Pretender* **Freddie Mercury**
2 *Stand By Me* **Ben E. King**
3 *Down To Earth* **Curiosity Killed The Cat**
4 *So Cold The Night* **The Communards**
5 *Jack Your Body* **Steve 'Silk' Hurley**
6 *I Love My Radio (Midnight Radio)* **Taffy**
7 *Loving You Is Sweeter Than Ever* **Nick Kamen**
8 *Manhattan Skyline* **a-ha**

Record 2 Side 2

1 *Sonic Boom Boy* **Westworld**
2 *Livin' On A Prayer* **Bon Jovi**
3 *Land Of Confusion* **Genesis**
4 *The Final Countdown* **Europe**
5 *Over The Hills And Far Away* **Gary Moore**
6 *Cross That Bridge* **The Ward Brothers**
7 *Hymn To Her* **The Pretenders**

▶ With 'So Cold The Night', **The Communards** landed their third of five *NOW* entries following *NOW 8*'s inclusion of 'Don't Leave Me This Way' – the biggest-selling UK single of 1986. Lead singer **Jimmy Somerville** would appear ten times across the first twenty editions of *NOW* – with **The Communards**, with **Bronski Beat** (*NOW 3* and *4*) and as a solo artist in his own right.

▶ **Steve 'Silk' Hurley** is a true UK one-hit wonder – a chart-topping introductory single, then nothing else, ever. He's the first we have met so far – there's another on *NOW 10* in the shape of 'Pump Up The Volume' by **M/A/R/R/S** and many more to come over the years.

30 TOP CHART HITS

NOW
THAT'S WHAT I CALL
music 10

M/A/R/R/S · PET SHOP BOYS · T'PAU · WET WET WET · THE COMMUNARDS · ERASURE · BILLY IDOL
KISS · HEART · CURIOSITY KILLED THE CAT · BANANARAMA · JOHNNY HATES JAZZ · LOS LOBOS
WHITESNAKE · NINA SIMONE · FREDDIE MERCURY AND MONTSERRAT CABALLÉ
PLUS MANY MORE

RELEASED 23 NOVEMBER 1987

**HELLO
WHITESNAKE

GOODBYE
MARILLION**

▶ The first of two entries for 'Barcelona' by **Freddie Mercury and Montserrat Caballé** – the next would appear posthumously on *NOW 23*. Between them, the members of **Queen** – either solo or collectively – have chalked up twenty appearances since *NOW 2*. Daaaaaay-oh!

CD1

1. *Barcelona* Freddie Mercury & Montserrat Caballé
2. *Rent* Pet Shop Boys
3. *Never Can Say Goodbye* The Communards
4. *Pump Up The Volume* M/A/R/R/S
5. *Labour Of Love* Hue And Cry
6. *The Real Thing* Jellybean feat. Steven Dante
7. *I Don't Want To Be A Hero* Johnny Hates Jazz
8. *Wanted* The Style Council
9. *China In Your Hand* T'Pau
10. *Alone* Heart
11. *Crazy Crazy Nights* Kiss
12. *Mony Mony* Billy Idol
13. *Here I Go Again* Whitesnake
14. *Rain In The Summertime* The Alarm
15. *Sugar Mice* Marillion

CD2

1. *Sweet Little Mystery* Wet Wet Wet
2. *Misfit* Curiosity Killed the Cat
3. *La Bamba* Los Lobos
4. *Wipe Out* The Beach Boys & The Fat Boys
5. *Love In The First Degree* Bananarama
6. *My Pretty One* Cliff Richard
7. *Hey Matthew* Karel Fialka
8. *Crockett's Theme* Jan Hammer
9. *My Baby Just Cares For Me* Nina Simone
10. *The Circus* Erasure
11. *Build* The Housemartins
12. *It's Over* Level 42
13. *When Smokey Sings* ABC
14. *Hourglass* Squeeze
15. *Fairytale Of New York* The Pogues feat. Kirsty MacColl

▶ **Hue and Cry**'s generous five-song *NOW* run is bookended by their biggest hit, 'Labour of Love'. Originally a No.6 hit in the UK, it also appeared on *NOW 24* in the form of a remixed version by **Joey Negro**. Dave Lee – the man behind the pseudonym – would appear on future *NOWs 48*, *51* and *53* under the nom de plume **Jakatta** and a second time on *NOW 53* as **Raven Maize**.

▶ 'My Pretty One' songwriter, producer and serial **Cliff Richard** collaborator Alan Tarney would go on to produce further acts such as **a-ha** (*NOW 9*), **Pulp** (*NOW 33*) and **Voice Of The Beehive** (*NOW 20*). His biggest worldwide songwriting hit remains 'We Don't Talk Anymore' for Cliff Richard, released prior to *NOW*'s 1983 inception.

NOW
THAT'S WHAT I CALL music 11

PET SHOP BOYS · WET WET WET · T'PAU · MEL & KIM · MORRISSEY
BELINDA CARLISLE · KYLIE MINOGUE · BILLY OCEAN · BOMB THE BASS · JERMAINE STEWART
BANANARAMA · EDDY GRANT · EDDIE COCHRAN · WHITESNAKE · JOHNNY HATES JAZZ · ELTON JOHN · THE MISSION
PLUS MANY MORE

RELEASED 21 MARCH 1988

**HELLO
KYLIE MINOGUE

GOODBYE
MEL & KIM**

▶ **Fine Young Cannibals** joined us on *NOW 5* and although there is a gap between appearances by them from *NOW 6* to *NOW 14*, David Steele and Andy Cox from the band are here using the alias **Two Men, a Drum Machine and a Trumpet**. The FYC guitarists made this one-off house record while lead singer Roland Gift pursued an acting career.

CD1

1 *Always On My Mind*
Pet Shop Boys

2 *Heaven Is A Place On Earth*
Belinda Carlisle

3 *Get Outta My Dreams,
Get Into My Car*
Billy Ocean

4 *Say It Again* **Jermaine Stewart**

5 *Gimme Hope Jo-anna*
Eddy Grant

6 *C'mon Everybody* **Eddie Cochran**

7 *Suedehead* **Morrissey**

8 *Candle In The Wind* **Elton John**

9 *Angel Eyes (Home And Away)*
Wet Wet Wet

10 *Turn Back The Clock*
Johnny Hates Jazz

11 *Valentine* **T'Pau**

12 *Hot In The City* **Billy Idol**

13 *Mandinka* **Sinéad O'Connor**

14 *Tower Of Strength* **The Mission**

15 *Give Me All Your Love* **Whitesnake**

CD2

1 *I Should Be So Lucky* **Kylie Minogue**

2 *That's The Way It Is* **Mel & Kim**

3 *Come Into My Life* **Joyce Sims**

4 *Who Found Who* **Jellybean feat.
Elisa Fiorillo**

5 *I Can't Help It* **Bananarama**

6 *Oh L'amour* **Dollar**

7 *Joe Le Taxi* **Vanessa Paradis**

8 *Stutter Rap (No Sleep Til
Bedtime)* **Morris Minor and
The Majors**

9 *Beat Dis* **Bomb The Bass**

10 *Doctorin' The House*
**Coldcut feat. Yazz & The
Plastic Population**

11 *House Arrest* **Krush**

12 *The Jack That House Built*
Jack 'N' Chill

13 *Rock Da House* **The Beatmasters
feat. Cookie Crew**

14 *I'm Tired Of Getting Pushed
Around* **Two Men A Drum Machine
And A Trumpet**

15 *Rise To The Occasion* **Climie Fisher**

▶ **Johnny Hates Jazz** wished they could 'Turn Back The Clock' and they aren't the only *NOW* hit-makers to have concerns about temporal matters. Over the years, 59 *NOW* titles have referenced time in some way, from **Cyndi Lauper's** 'Time After Time' (*NOW 3*) to **Sub Focus** and their attempt to 'Turn Back Time' on *NOW 87*. The only band to join **Johnny Hates Jazz** in some ticktock scrutiny was **Coldplay** ('Clocks', *NOW 54*).

▶ The early 1988 rise to prominence of UK-based house producers was healthily represented by **Bomb The Bass**, **Coldcut** and **The Beatmasters**. All would go on to assist with hits for other artists, respectively: **Björk & David Arnold** ('Play Dead', *NOW 26*); **Yazz & The Plastic Population** ('The Only Way Is Up', *NOW 13*) and **Aswad** ('Shine', *NOW 28*). Meanwhile Mark Brydon of **Krush** would go on to become half of *NOW 44* and *45* stars **Moloko**.

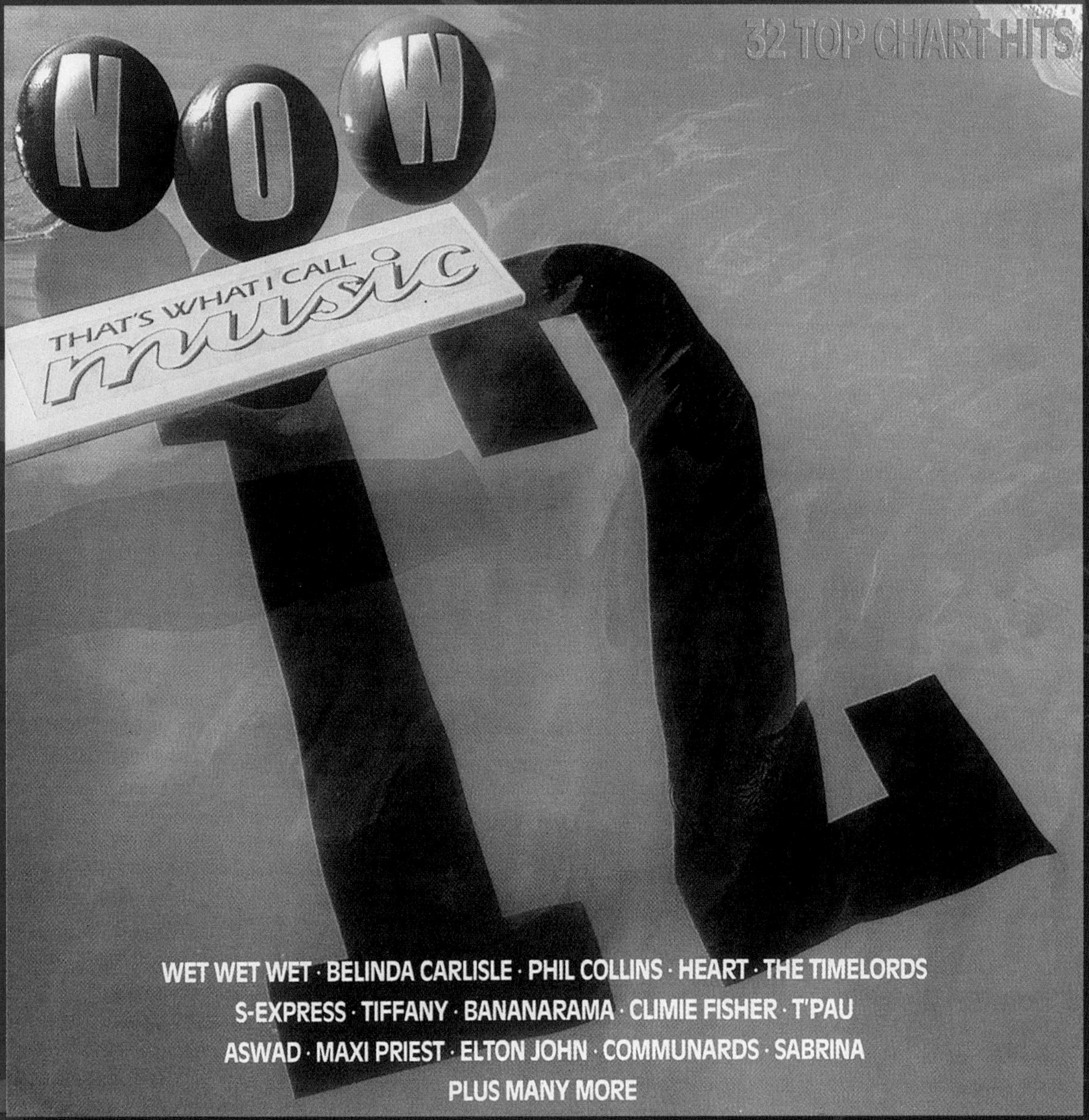

NOW
THAT'S WHAT I CALL music
11

WET WET WET · BELINDA CARLISLE · PHIL COLLINS · HEART · THE TIMELORDS
S-EXPRESS · TIFFANY · BANANARAMA · CLIMIE FISHER · T'PAU
ASWAD · MAXI PRIEST · ELTON JOHN · COMMUNARDS · SABRINA
PLUS MANY MORE

RELEASED 11 JULY 1988

HELLO
SALT 'N' PEPA
GOODBYE
JERMAINE STEWART

▶ **Bananarama** still hold the world record for female group with most global chart entries, yet here we found them towards the end of their eight-strong *NOW* run and their penultimate Top 10 hit with founding member Siobhan Fahey. Fahey would return to the *NOW* fold with **Shakespears Sister** on *NOW 16*, appearing three times in total.

CD1

1. *With A Little Help From My Friends* Wet Wet Wet
2. *Circle In The Sand* Belinda Carlisle
3. *Wild World* Maxi Priest
4. *Give A Little Love* Aswad
5. *Love Changes (Everything)* Climie Fisher
6. *I Don't Wanna Go On With You Like That* Elton John
7. *Oh Patti (Don't Feel Sorry For Loverboy)* Scritti Politti
8. *In The Air Tonight* Phil Collins
9. *Don't Go* The Hothouse Flowers
10. *Everyday Is Like Sunday* Morrissey
11. *Mary's Prayer* Danny Wilson
12. *Heart Of Gold* Johnny Hates Jazz
13. *Don't Call Me Baby* Voice of the Beehive
14. *Can I Play With Madness* Iron Maiden
15. *These Dreams* Heart
16. *I Will Be With You* T'Pau

CD2

1. *Doctorin' The Tardis* The Timelords
2. *Boys (Summertime Love)* Sabrina
3. *I Want You Back* Bananarama
4. *I Think We're Alone Now* Tiffany
5. *Who's Leaving Who* Hazell Dean
6. *There's More To Love Than Boy Meets Girl* The Communards
7. *Get Lucky* Jermaine Stewart
8. *Nothing's Gonna Change My Love For You* Glenn Medeiros
9. *Theme From S-Express* S-Express
10. *Push It* Salt 'N' Pepa
11. *Bad Young Brother* Derek B
12. *The Payback Mix (Part One)* James Brown
13. *Car Wash* Rose Royce
14. *Pink Cadillac* Natalie Cole
15. *Just A Mirage* Jellybean feat. Adele Bertei
16. *A Love Supreme* Will Downing

▶ Jazz legends ahoy! *NOW 12* featured **Will Downing**'s R&B cover of John Coltrane's 'A Love Supreme', alongside bebop hornsmith **Miles Davis** who blew some cool brass notes on **Scritti Politti**'s 'Oh Patti (Don't Feel Sorry For Loverboy)'. Impudently cocking a snook at their illustrious forebears on this volume, **Johnny Hates Jazz** drew the curtains on their bijou three-song consecutive run.

▶ The first of two appearances for Tommy James & The Shondells' 'I Think We're Alone Now' was a UK No.1 for **Tiffany** in early 1988. Fifty-four volumes later, **Girls Aloud** would place their own version on *NOW 66* – their fourteenth consecutive Top 10 hit and fourteenth consecutive *NOW* appearance. The first Tommy James cover to feature on a *NOW*, however, was 'Mony Mony' by **Billy Idol** on *NOW 10*.

YAZZ · BROTHER BEYOND · PHIL COLLINS · SALT 'N' PEPA · KIM WILDE · DURAN DURAN
ROBERT PALMER · BOBBY McFERRIN · BRYAN FERRY · LEVEL 42 · ERASURE · THE HOLLIES
UB40 with CHRISSIE HYNDE · FAT BOYS · ART OF NOISE featuring TOM JONES
PLUS MANY MORE

RELEASED 21 NOVEMBER 1988

**HELLO
TOM JONES

GOODBYE
T'PAU**

▶ Long-running electronic mavericks **Yello** got to the *NOW* finishing line with 'The Race' and in so doing became the first Swiss act to feature. *NOW 29* star **Celine Dion** won the 1988 Eurovision Song Contest representing Switzerland, but is Canadian born and bred.

CD1

1. *The Only Way Is Up* Yazz & The Plastic Population
2. *Teardrops* Womack & Womack
3. *A Little Respect* Erasure
4. *Harvest For The World* The Christians
5. *Ordinary Angel* Hue And Cry
6. *Breakfast In Bed* UB40 feat. Chrissie Hynde
7. *She Makes My Day* Robert Palmer
8. *Hands To Heaven* Breathe
9. *A Groovy Kind Of Love* Phil Collins
10. *Don't Worry, Be Happy* Bobby McFerrin
11. *Kiss* Art of Noise feat. Tom Jones
12. *Let's Stick Together* Bryan Ferry
13. *You Came* Kim Wilde
14. *Don't Make Me Wait* Bomb the Bass
15. *The Harder I Try* Brother Beyond
16. *He Ain't Heavy, He's My Brother* The Hollies

CD2

1. *The Twist (Yo Twist)* The Fat Boys & Chubby Checker
2. *Wee Rule* The Wee Papa Girl Rappers
3. *Twist And Shout* Salt 'N' Pepa
4. *The Race* Yello
5. *Big Fun* Inner City feat. Kevin Saunderson
6. *We Call It Acieed* D-Mob & Gary Haisman
7. *Burn It Up* The Beatmasters & P.P. Arnold
8. *Girl You Know It's True* Milli Vanilli
9. *Heaven In My Hands* Level 42
10. *Rush Hour* Jane Wiedlin
11. *I'm Gonna Be (500 Miles)* The Proclaimers
12. *Secret Garden* T'Pau
13. *I Want Your Love* Transvision Vamp
14. *I Don't Want Your Love* Duran Duran
15. *Love Is All That Matters* The Human League
16. *Martha's Harbour* All About Eve

▶ It was a good *NOW* for the older artist: **Chubby Checker** had been having UK hits since 1960, while **Tom Jones** first charted in 1965 and **P.P. Arnold** made her last appearance in 1967. All returned here in the company of younger performers. **The Hollies** (first hit: 1963) needed no outside assistance, however, and placed their 1969 recording 'He Ain't Heavy, He's My Brother' at No.1 and on *NOW 13* thanks to its prominence in a TV ad-campaign for beer.

▶ **Milli Vanilli** appeared on two *NOW* albums with 'Girl You Know It's True' and 'Girl I'm Gonna Miss You' before being enveloped in controversy when it emerged that the two gentlemen in the videos and on *Top Of The Pops* did not actually sing on the records. After the furore had died down, the ensuing **Milli Vanilli** single pictured the four session singers whose vocals could be heard on the sleeve. It wasn't a hit.

MARC ALMOND featuring GENE PITNEY · PHIL COLLINS · ERASURE
BANANARAMA/LANANEENEENOONOO · YAZZ · SIMPLE MINDS · ROY ORBISON · PAULA ABDUL
BROTHER BEYOND · S'XPRESS · KIM WILDE · INXS
PLUS MANY MORE

RELEASED 20 MARCH 1989

HELLO
NENEH CHERRY
GOODBYE
THE STYLE COUNCIL

▶ In January 1989 **Samantha Fox** became the fourth artist to place 'I Only Wanna Be With You' inside the UK Top 40. **Dusty Springfield**'s 1963 original, the Bay City Rollers' version in 1976 and The Tourists' cover in 1979 all reached No.4. Sam Fox's release stalled at No.16 which, tenuously, is still four squared.

CD1

1. *Something's Gotten Hold Of My Heart* **Marc Almond feat. Gene Pitney**
2. *Two Hearts* **Phil Collins**
3. *Stop!* **Erasure**
4. *Help!* **Bananarama**
5. *Looking For Linda* **Hue And Cry**
6. *Fine Time* **Yazz**
7. *Four Letter Word* **Kim Wilde**
8. *Stop* **Sam Brown**
9. *You Got It* **Roy Orbison**
10. *She Drives Me Crazy* **Fine Young Cannibals**
11. *Need You Tonight* **INXS**
12. *Burning Bridges (On And Off And On Again)* **Status Quo**
13. *Big Area* **Then Jerico**
14. *The Last Of The Famous International Playboys* **Morrissey**
15. *Every Rose Has Its Thorn* **Poison**
16. *Belfast Child* **Simple Minds**

CD2

1. *Buffalo Stance* **Neneh Cherry**
2. *Good Life* **Inner City**
3. *Hey Music Lover* **S-Express**
4. *Blow The House Down* **Living in a Box**
5. *Promised Land* **The Style Council**
6. *Respect* **Adeva**
7. *Wild Thing* **Tone Lōc**
8. *I Live For Your Love* **Natalie Cole**
9. *First Time* **Robin Beck**
10. *Straight Up* **Paula Abdul**
11. *I Only Wanna Be With You* **Samantha Fox**
12. *Be My Twin* **Brother Beyond**
13. *Love Like A River* **Climie Fisher**
14. *All She Wants Is* **Duran Duran**
15. *Tracie* **Level 42**
16. *Love Changes Everything* **Michael Ball**

▶ A debut songwriting appearance for Andrew Lloyd Webber penning **Michael Ball**'s 'Love Changes Everything' for the musical *Aspects Of Love*. The West End lord would crop up again having written for **Jason Donovan** (*NOW 20*), **Dina Carroll** (*NOW 27*) and **Boyzone** (*NOW 41*). Lloyd Webber was also the Svengali behind **Doctor Spin** (*NOW 23*) and, alongside crazed children's TV presenter Timmy Mallet, **Bombalurina** (*NOW 18*).

▶ 'You Got It' marks the first of three appearances for the legendary Big O, **Roy Orbison**. Although co-written by Jeff Lynne and Tom Petty, Orbison remains the only credited Travelling Wilbury to appear on a *NOW* release. Their fellow bandmates – Bob Dylan and George Harrison – also remain unchronicled by *NOW*, although Dylan's 'Make You Feel My Love' provides **Adele** with her breakout hit on *NOW 77*.

32 TOP CHART HITS

NOW

THAT'S WHAT I CALL *music*

15

QUEEN · SIMPLE MINDS · FINE YOUNG CANNIBALS · PAUL McCARTNEY
SOUL II SOUL featuring CARON WHEELER · BOBBY BROWN · NENEH CHERRY · PET SHOP BOYS
NATALIE COLE · CLIFF RICHARD · TRANSVISION VAMP
JIVE BUNNY AND THE MASTERMIXERS
PLUS MANY MORE

RELEASED 14 AUGUST 1989

HELLO
SOUL II SOUL
GOODBYE
NATALIE COLE

▶ **Stevie Nicks**'s first and highest charting UK Top 40 solo single is included on this edition of *NOW*, yet it would be another twenty-four years before her **Fleetwood Mac** contemporaries made their first – and to date – last appearance: on *NOW 84* with a re-promoted 'Everywhere'.

CD1

1 *I Want It All* Queen
2 *Kick It In* Simple Minds
3 *Good Thing* Fine Young Cannibals
4 *Americanos* Holly Johnson
5 *Baby I Don't Care* Transvision Vamp
6 *Mystify* INXS
7 *The Look* Roxette
8 *Rooms On Fire* Stevie Nicks
9 *My Brave Face* Paul McCartney
10 *Ferry Cross The Mersey* Gerry Marsden/Paul McCartney/Holly Johnson and The Christians
11 *Song For Whoever* The Beautiful South
12 *Days* Kirsty MacColl
13 *The Second Summer Of Love* Danny Wilson
14 *Cry* Waterfront
15 *Violently* Hue and Cry
16 *The Best Of Me* Cliff Richard

CD2

1 *Back To Life (However Do You Want Me)* Soul II Soul feat. Caron Wheeler
2 *Manchild* Neneh Cherry
3 *Every Little Step* Bobby Brown
4 *Do You Love What You Feel* Inner City
5 *It Is Time To Get Funky* D-Mob feat. LRS
6 *Joy And Pain* Donna Allen
7 *Licence To Kill* Gladys Knight
8 *Miss You Like Crazy* Natalie Cole
9 *It's Alright* Pet Shop Boys
10 *Swing The Mood* Jive Bunny & The Music Mixers
11 *You On My Mind* Swing Out Sister
12 *Cruel Summer* Bananarama
13 *Say No Go* De La Soul
14 *Blame It On The Bassline* Norman Cook & MC Wildski
15 *Just Keep Rockin'* Double Trouble & The Rebel MC
16 *Lullaby* The Cure

▶ **The Beautiful South** have, to date, had eleven songs on *NOW*s, with singer Paul Heaton also contributing to the four times **The Housemartins** made it into the tracklistings in the '80s. Fellow Housemartin **Norman Cook**, who made his solo debut here, also crops up later on as a member of **Beats International** (*NOW 17*), of **Freak Power** (*NOW 30*) and five times as alter ego **Fatboy Slim**.

▶ Former frontman of four-time stars **Frankie Goes To Hollywood**, **Holly Johnson** popped up twice on *NOW 15*: solo with 'Americanos' and on the charity single 'Ferry Cross The Mersey'. This is the only edition on which he appeared under his own name. **Paul McCartney** also placed two songs on this *NOW* after performing on 'Ferry Cross The Mersey' and his appearances are consecutive on the tracklisting.

NOW 16 THAT'S WHAT I CALL music

TEARS FOR FEARS · WET WET WET · ERASURE · BELINDA CARLISLE
THE BEAUTIFUL SOUTH · TINA TURNER · QUEEN · LIVING IN A BOX
MILLI VANILLI · ADEVA · BOBBY BROWN · RICHARD MARX
PLUS MANY MORE

RELEASED 20 NOVEMBER 1989

HELLO
RICHARD MARX

GOODBYE
FINE YOUNG
CANNIBALS

▶ Tina Turner's 'The Best' marks her sixth appearance in six years, the single was a flop twelve months earlier for French navigational nightmare **Bonnie Tyler**. Songwriter Mike Chapman – of 'Chinn & Chapman' fame – would return with **Ace of Base** on *NOW 42*.

CD1

1 *Sowing The Seeds Of Love* **Tears for Fears**
2 *Leave A Light On* **Belinda Carlisle**
3 *Drama!* **Erasure**
4 *I Want That Man* **Deborah Harry**
5 *If Only I Could* **Sydney Youngblood**
6 *Name And Number* **Curiosity Killed The Cat**
7 *You Keep It All In* **The Beautiful South**
8 *Sweet Surrender* **Wet Wet Wet**
9 *Breakthru* **Queen**
10 *The Best* **Tina Turner**
11 *Born To Be Sold* **Transvision Vamp**
12 *Waterfall '89* **Wendy & Lisa**
13 *The Sensual World* **Kate Bush**
14 *I'm Not The Man I Used To Be* **Fine Young Cannibals**
15 *Sugarbox* **Then Jerico**
16 *Room In Your Heart* **Living in a Box**
17 *Right Here Waiting* **Richard Marx**
18 *Girl I'm Gonna Miss You* **Milli Vanilli**

CD2

1 *Street Tuff* **Rebel MC & Double Trouble**
2 *On Our Own* **Bobby Brown**
3 *Pump Up The Jam* **Technotronic feat. Felly**
4 *French Kiss* **Lil Louis**
5 *I Thank You* **Adeva**
6 *C'Mon And Get My Love* **D-Mob feat. Cathy Dennis**
7 *Eye Know* **De La Soul**
8 *Whatcha Gonna Do With My Lovin'* **Inner City**
9 *Can't Shake The Feeling* **Big Fun**
10 *I Just Don't Have The Heart* **Cliff Richard**
11 *Comment Te Dire Adieu?* **Jimmy Somerville feat. June Miles Kingston**
12 *Drive On* **Brother Beyond**
13 *You're History* **Shakespears Sister**
14 *Oh Well* **Oh Well**
15 *Kisses On The Wind* **Neneh Cherry**
16 *Do The Right Thing* **Redhead Kingpin & The FBI**
17 *Wishing On A Star* **Fresh 4 feat. Lizz E**

▶ **Wendy & Lisa** would beat their former employer **Prince** to a *NOW* debut by two years and four volumes ('Gett Off' on *NOW 20* opening Prince's account). That said, 'Waterfall '89' was an unusual *NOW* misstep, peaking at No.69 in the UK singles chart.

▶ Although 'C'Mon And Get My Love' marked the penultimate *NOW* soft-shoe shuffle for **D-Mob**, guest vocalist **Cathy Dennis** was only just warming up. Two performer appearances followed (*NOW 20* and *36*) but her subsequent songwriting career would result in a plethora of future pop classics: 'Reach' (**S Club 7**, *NOW 46*), 'Can't Get You Out Of My Head' (**Kylie**, *NOW 50*), 'About You Now' (**Sugababes**, *NOW 68*) and 'I Kissed A Girl' (**Katy Perry**, *NOW 71*).

32 TOP CHART HITS

NOW

THAT'S WHAT I CALL
MUSIC 17

FEATURING

ERASURE · PAULA ABDUL · PHIL COLLINS · UB40 · TINA TURNER
BEATS INTERNATIONAL · HAPPY MONDAYS · DEPECHE MODE
TECHNOTRONIC · BIZZ NIZZ · CANDY FLIP · REBEL MC
PLUS MANY MORE

RELEASED 23 APRIL 1990

**HELLO
SEAL**

**GOODBYE
CLIFF RICHARD**

▶ **Phil Collins** appeared here as both a performer ('I Wish It Would Rain Down', with a guitar solo from an uncredited **Eric Clapton**) and as a songwriter, although how he feels about **Jam Tronik**'s idiosyncratic Eurodance version of 'Another Day In Paradise' is unknown at the time of going to press.

CD1

1 *Blue Savannah* **Erasure**
2 *Better World* **Rebel MC**
3 *Opposites Attract* **Paula Abdul**
4 *Dub Be Good To Me* **Beats International feat. Lindy Layton**
5 *Kingston Town* **UB40**
6 *Strawberry Fields Forever* **Candy Flip**
7 *I Don't Wanna Lose You* **Tina Turner**
8 *I Wish It Would Rain Down* **Phil Collins**
9 *Step On* **Happy Mondays**
10 *Loaded* **Primal Scream**
11 *Enjoy The Silence* **Depeche Mode**
12 *Real Real Real* **Jesus Jones**
13 *This Is How It Feels* **Inspiral Carpets**
14 *Shine On* **House Of Love**
15 *From Out Of Nowhere* **Faith No More**
16 *Hey You* **The Quireboys**

CD2

1 *This Beat Is Technotronic* **Technotronic feat. MC Eric**
2 *Happenin' All Over Again* **Lonnie Gordon**
3 *Don't You Love Me* **The 49ers**
4 *Read My Lips (Enough Is Enough)* **Jimmy Somerville**
5 *Stronger Than That* **Cliff Richard**
6 *Another Day In Paradise* **Jam Tronik**
7 *Moments In Soul* **J.T. & The Big Family**
8 *Got To Have Your Love* **Mantronix feat. Wondress**
9 *Don't Miss The Partyline* **Bizz Nizz**
10 *Everything Starts With An 'E'* **E-Zee Possee feat. MC Kinky**
11 *Put Your Hands Together* **D-Mob feat. Nuff Juice**
12 *Killer* **Adamski feat. Seal**
13 *Chime* **Orbital**
14 *Tomorrow* **Tongue 'N' Cheek**
15 *Talking With Myself* **Electribe 101**
16 *I'd Rather Go Blind* **Sydney Youngblood**

▶ Fifth-letter-of-the-alphabet obsessives **E-Zee Possee feat. MC Kinky** hid a star name in their ranks. 'Everything Starts With An 'E'' co-writer, Angela Dust, was in reality *NOW 9* and **Culture Club** veteran **Boy George** using a pseudonym. He would appear again on *NOW 19* as **Jesus Loves You**. Possee member **MC Kinky** would later contribute to **Erasure**'s chart topping version of **Abba**'s 'Take A Chance On Me'.

▶ 'Opposites Attract' was the second of four *NOW* entries for **Paula Abdul** and the song is now more commonly remembered for the video and her animated dance partner **MC Skat Kat**. Slightly misjudging the public's appetite for subsequent stand-alone **MC Skat Kat** material, an album was nonetheless released in 1991. The sole single – 'Skat Strut' – reached No.9 in Norway.

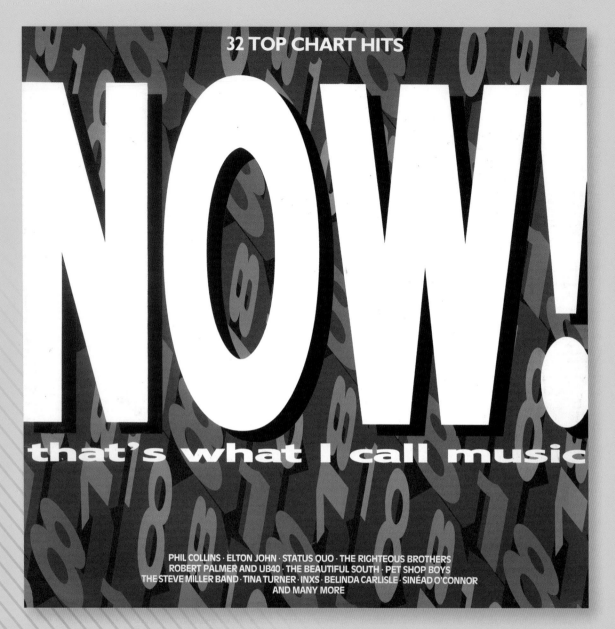

32 TOP CHART HITS

NOW!
that's what I call music

PHIL COLLINS · ELTON JOHN · STATUS QUO · THE RIGHTEOUS BROTHERS
ROBERT PALMER AND UB40 · THE BEAUTIFUL SOUTH · PET SHOP BOYS
THE STEVE MILLER BAND · TINA TURNER · INXS · BELINDA CARLISLE · SINÉAD O'CONNOR
AND MANY MORE

RELEASED 19 NOVEMBER 1990

HELLO
MC HAMMER
GOODBYE
SINÉAD O'CONNOR

▶ 'The Joker' by the **Steve Miller Band** represents the first and only time a song has reached No.1 on a technicality ruling. Both it and 'Groove Is In The Heart' by **Deee-Lite** sold the exact same number of copies that week but Miller assumed the No.1 position having witnessed a larger week-on-week sales growth.

CD1

1 *A Little Time* The Beautiful South
2 *The Joker* Steve Miller Band
3 *Sacrifice* Elton John
4 *It Must Have Been Love* Roxette
5 *Something Happened On The Way To Heaven* Phil Collins
6 *Hold On* Wilson Phillips
7 *Nothing Compares 2 U* Sinéad O'Connor
8 *Unchained Melody* Righteous Brothers
9 *(We Want) The Same Thing* Belinda Carlisle
10 *The Anniversary Waltz (Part One)* Status Quo
11 *Suicide Blonde* INXS
12 *Don't Ask Me* Public Image Ltd
13 *It's My Life* Talk Talk
14 *There She Goes* The La's
15 *Be Tender With Me Baby* Tina Turner
16 *I'll Be Your Baby Tonight* Robert Palmer feat. UB40

CD2

1 *So Hard* Pet Shop Boys
2 *Fascinating Rhythm* Bass-O-Matic
3 *Missing You* Soul II Soul feat. Kym Mazelle
4 *Tom's Diner* DNA feat. Suzanne Vega
5 *Englishman In New York* Sting
6 *Close To You Remix* The Cure
7 *I've Got You Under My Skin* Neneh Cherry
8 *Little Brother* Blue Pearl
9 *Step Back In Time* Kylie Minogue
10 *Don't Worry* Kim Appleby
11 *Megamix* Technotronic
12 *Itsy Bitsy Teenie Weenie Yellow Polka Dot Bikini* Bombalurina
13 *Where Are You Baby?* Betty Boo
14 *Dirty Cash (Money Talks)* The Adventures of Stevie V
15 *Have You Seen Her* MC Hammer
16 *To Love Somebody* Jimmy Somerville

▶ Our old friends **UB40** have a *NOW* career spanning twenty years and thirteen appearances, including a remarkable seven entries across the first ten *NOW*s – more than any other artist. Ten of these tracks – including 'Kingston Town' featured here – were cover versions of songs made famous by artists as diverse as Bob Dylan, Neil Diamond and Winston Groovy, none of whom have appeared on a *NOW* in their own right.

▶ 'Unchained Melody', re-released to coincide with the hit film *Ghost*, is the only song chronicled by *NOW* to have been No.1 in the UK in four different versions, as well as having sold over a million copies in three of those iterations. Robson & Jerome (1995), **Gareth Gates** (2002) and the **Righteous Brothers** (1990) make up the million selling club, while Jimmy Young (1955) completes the quartet of hit-makers.

LIVE AID
13 JULY 1985
THE DAY IN *NOW* ARTIST APPEARANCES

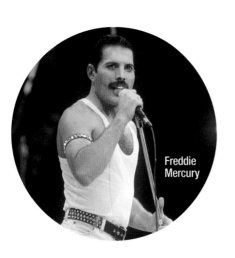
Freddie Mercury

Chart data (artist: appearances):

- Status Quo: 6
- Style Council: 5
- Boomtown Rats: 0
- Adam Ant: 0
- Ultravox: 2
- Spandau Ballet: 0
- Elvis Costello: 0
- Nik Kershaw: 4
- Sade: 1
- Sting: 2
- Phil Collins: 13
- Howard Jones: 4
- Bryan Ferry: 3
- Paul Young: 3
- U2: 19
- Dire Straits: 0
- Queen: 13
- David Bowie: 3
- The Who: 0
- Elton John: 10
- Freddie Mercury: 4
- Brian May: 3
- Paul McCartney: 7

now!

at's what i call music

CHRIS REA · OLETA ADAMS · CHRIS ISAAK · THE CLASH
EMF · ROBERT PALMER · KIM APPLEBY · FREE
MC HAMMER · QUEEN · THE KLF · INXS · SEAL
AND MANY MORE

ED 25 MARCH 1991

HELLO
SIVE ATTACK

OODBYE
TTI POLITTI

▶ Only two artists on the tracklisting of *NOW 19* can point to having made it to double figures in terms of appearances – **Kylie Minogue** has placed twenty-three songs on twenty-three *NOW*s in twenty-three years from 1988 to 2010, while **Queen**'s 'Innuendo' was the last song of theirs to hit No.1 while lead singer **Freddie Mercury** was still alive.

THE BRITPOP APPEARANCE PIE

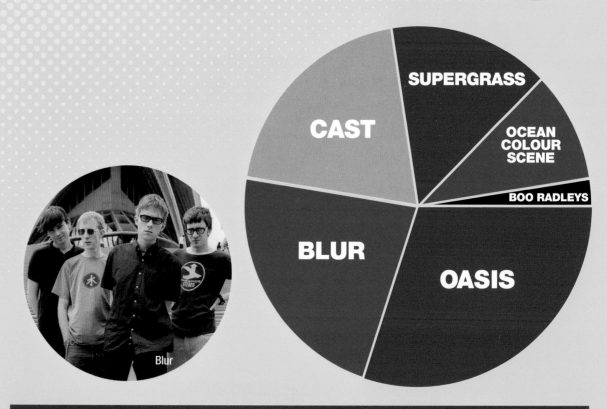

SUPERGRASS

CAST

OCEAN
COLOUR
SCENE

BOO RADLEYS

BLUR

OASIS

Blur

MADCHESTER RAVES ON... SORT OF

APPEARANCES

7 James

2 New Order

1 Happy Mondays, 808 State, Inspiral Carpets, Candy Flip, The Beloved

0 Stone Roses, The Charlatans, Northside, MC Tunes

New Order

WE SALUTE...
THE MAJESTY OF COLLINS

67 SPREAD OF APPEARANCES SPANNING *NOW 1 – NOW 68*

13 ENTRIES AS A SOLO ARTIST

7 ENTRIES WITH GENESIS

5 ENTRIES TAKEN FROM A FILM SOUNDTRACK

2 SEPARATE APPEARANCES FOR 'IN THE AIR TONIGHT'

2 SEPARATE APPEARANCES FOR 'INVISIBLE TOUCH'

FAB! A COLLECTIO OF BEATLES

With A Little Help From My Friends
WET WET WET

Twist
CHA
& F

Twist & Shout
SALT 'N' PEPA

Help
BANANARAMA

Strawberry Fields Forever
CANDY FLIP

She's A Woman
SCRITTI POLITTI FEAT. SHABBA RANKS

RELEAS

MASS

G
SCRI

TRACKLISTING NOW 19

CD1

1 *Should I Stay Or Should I Go*
   The Clash
2 *She's A Woman* Scritti Politti feat.
   Shabba Ranks
3 *You Got The Love* The Source feat.
   Candi Staton
4 *3 AM Eternal (Live At The SSL)*
   The KLF feat. The Children
   of the Revolution
5 *Gonna Make You Sweat (Everybody
   Dance Now)* C&C Music Factory
6 *(I Wanna Give You) Devotion*
   Nomad feat. MC Mikee Freedom
7 *I Believe* EMF
8 *In Yer Face* 808 State
9 *Unfinished Sympathy*
   Massive
10 *Pray* M C Hammer
11 *G.L.A.D.* Kim Appleby
12 *What Do I Have To Do*
   Kylie Minogue
13 *The Stonk* Hale & Pace
   & The Stonkers
14 *Wiggle It* 2 In A Room
15 *Play That Funky Music* Vanilla Ice
16 *Bow Down Mister* Jesus Loves You
17 *Sadeness (Part 1)* Enigma
18 *Only You* Praise

CD2

1 *Get Here* Oleta Adams
2 *Cry For Help* Rick Astley
3 *Mercy Mercy Me/I Want You*
   Robert Palmer
4 *(I've Had) The Time Of My Life*
   Bill Medley & Jennifer Warnes
5 *You've Lost That Lovin' Feelin'*
   Righteous Brothers
6 *Crazy* Seal
7 *This Is Your Life* Banderas
8 *Because I Love You (The Postman
   Song)* Stevie B
9 *Auberge* Chris Rea
10 *Blue Hotel* Chris Isaak
11 *All Right Now* Free
12 *Disappear* INXS
13 *Summer Rain* Belinda Carlisle
14 *Every Beat Of The Heart*
   The Railway Children
15 *Love Walked In* Thunder
16 *Innuendo* Queen

▶ Elsewhere on this edition, there are eighteen artists who only ever appeared in the *NOW* series once – a new high that would not be surpassed until *NOW 46* nine years later. Not all of them could be described as one-hit wonders though – such chart luminaries as **The Clash, Chris Rea, Rick Astley** and **Free** are all here, along with less remembered artists **Praise, 2 In A Room** and **Stevie B**.

▶ Much-missed art-pop malcontents **The KLF** made the most of their brief *NOW* time span. Making their debut under this name here, they would notch two appearances on *NOW 21* and in between find time for their alter egos, **The Justified Ancients Of Mu Mu**, to inform us 'It's Grim Up North' on *NOW 20*. Previously, as **The Timelords**, they were 'Doctorin' The Tardis' on *NOW 12*.

NOW THAT'S WHAT I CALL MUSIC! 20

HELLO
2 UNLIMITED
GOODBYE
PAUL YOUNG

▶ An uncredited vocal appearance from **Rod Stewart** propelled **Glass Tiger**'s one hit 'My Town' into the charts and on to *NOW 20*. It was Rod's first appearance since 'Baby Jane' on the inaugural volume of *NOW* in 1983. His last – to date – was an **N-Trance** cover version of 'Da Ya Think I'm Sexy' on *NOW 38*.

TRACKLISTING NOW 20

CD1

1 *Dizzy* Vic Reeves & The Wonderstuff
2 *Live Your Life Be Free* Belinda Carlisle
3 *The Fly* U2
4 *Where The Streets Have No Name (I Can't Take My Eyes Off You)* Pet Shop Boys
5 *Love To Hate You* Erasure
6 *Sailing On The Seven Seas* Orchestral Manoeuvres in the Dark
7 *Something Got Me Started* Simply Red
8 *Change* Lisa Stansfield
9 *Sunshine On A Rainy Day* Zoë
10 *Let's Talk About Sex* Salt 'N' Pepa
11 *I Wanna Sex You Up* Color Me Badd
12 *Best Of You* Kenny Thomas
13 *Gett Off* Prince & The New Power Generation
14 *Faith (In The Power Of Love)* Rozalla
15 *Get Ready For This* 2 Unlimited
16 *Go* Moby
17 *It's Grim Up North* The Justified Ancients of Mu Mu
18 *Set Adrift On Memory Bliss* PM Dawn

CD2

1 *Don't Dream It's Over* Paul Young
2 *Caribbean Blue* Enya
3 *Saltwater* Julian Lennon
4 *Rush, Rush* Paula Abdul
5 *Any Dream Will Do* Jason Donovan
6 *Too Many Walls* Cathy Dennis
7 *This House* Alison Moyet
8 *Walking In Memphis* Marc Cohen
9 *My Town* Glass Tiger
10 *Wind Of Change* Scorpions
11 *Shining Star* INXS
12 *Joyride* Roxette
13 *Sit Down* James
14 *I Think I Love You* Voice of the Beehive
15 *Radio Wall Of Sound* Slade
16 *Always Look On The Bright Side Of Life* Monty Python
17 *American Pie* Don McLean

▶ UK glam-rock veterans **Slade** scored an unlikely hit single in 1991 with this track promoting their new *Best of...* album. It was their first *NOW* entry since 'Run Runaway' on *NOW 2* and their last to date. The single also features an unlikely vocal cameo from Radio 1 DJ Mike Read.

▶ Spandau Ballet never appeared on a numbered *NOW* release so **P.M. Dawn**'s sampling of 'True' on their Top 3 hit 'Set Adrift On Memory Bliss' is the closest Gary, Martin, John, Steve and Big Tone get to *NOW* club membership. PM Dawn, however, would appear again on *NOW 24* with the single 'Looking Through Patient Eyes'.

RELEASED 13 APRIL 1992

HELLO
DIANA ROSS

GOODBYE
MC HAMMER

▶ **Alison Limerick** is beloved of house music fans to this day for 'Make It On My Own' and 'Where Love Lives' but comedy fans may be unaware she is one of the uncredited voices singing over the end credits of the 1987 series *Blackadder the Third*.

TRACKLISTING NOW 21

CD1

1. *Bohemian Rhapsody* **Queen**
2. *Goodnight Girl* **Wet Wet Wet**
3. *Stay* **Shakespears Sister**
4. *My Girl* **The Temptations**
5. *Stars* **Simply Red**
6. *Justified & Ancient* **The KLF feat. Tammy Wynette**
7. *It Must Be Love* **Madness**
8. *I Can't Dance* **Genesis**
9. *(Love Moves In) Mysterious Ways* **Julia Fordham**
10. *Weather With You* **Crowded House**
11. *Deeply Dippy* **Right Said Fred**
12. *To Be With You* **Mr. Big**
13. *Love Is Strange* **Everything But The Girl**
14. *Church Of Your Heart* **Roxette**
15. *Driven By You* **Brian May**
16. *Welcome To The Cheap Seats* **The Wonder Stuff**
17. *Far Gone And Out* **The Jesus and Mary Chain**
18. *Born Of Frustration* **James**
19. *High* **The Cure**

CD2

1. *I Love Your Smile* **Shanice**
2. *I'm Doing Fine Now* **The Pasadenas**
3. *Give Me Just A Little More Time* **Kylie Minogue**
4. *Ride Like The Wind* **East Side Beat**
5. *Twilight Zone* **2 Unlimited**
6. *America: What Time Is Love?* **The KLF feat. The Children of the Revolution**
7. *A Deeper Love* **Clivilles & Cole**
8. *It's A Fine Day* **Opus III**
9. *Breath Of Life* **Erasure**
10. *Addams Groove* **Hammer**
11. *Expression* **Salt 'N' Pepa**
12. *We Got A Love Thang* **Ce Ce Peniston**
13. *Vibeology* **Paula Abdul**
14. *Make It On My Own* **Alison Limerick**
15. *Way Of The World* **Tina Turner**
16. *I Wonder Why* **Curtis Stigers**
17. *When You Tell Me That You Love Me* **Diana Ross**

▶With 'Deeply Dippy', **Right Said Fred** finally made it to the summit of the UK chart – a feat also matched by its parent album *Up*. 'I'm Too Sexy' had reached No.2 the previous summer and was held there for six weeks by **Bryan Adams's** '(Everything I Do) I Do It For You'. One further *NOW* entry – 'Wonderman' (*NOW 27*, 1994) – stalled at a rather lowlier No.55.

▶Three of the first seven tracks on *NOW 21* pre-dated the *NOW* series in age terms: **Queen's** 'Bohemian Rhapsody' initially charted in 1975, 'My Girl' was first a hit in 1965 for **The Temptations** and **Madness's** 'It Must Be Love' originally made it to the shops in 1981. Elsewhere there were covers of hit songs from 1970 ('Give Me Just A Little More Time', 1973 ('I'm Doing Fine Now') and 1980 ('Ride Like The Wind').

RELEASED 27 JULY 1992

HELLO
GEORGE MICHAEL

GOODBYE
THE CURE

▶ **SL2** reached No.2 with their 'On A Ragga Tip' which marked the first *NOW* entry for XL Recordings, who would later achieve global ubiquity with **Adele** (five *NOW* appearances to date, debuting on *NOW 69*).

CD1

1   *Take A Chance On Me* Erasure
2   *Finally* Ce Ce Peniston
3   *Please Don't Go* KWS
4   *It Only Takes A Minute* Take That
5   *Heartbeat* Nick Berry
6   *Rhythm Is A Dancer* Snap!
7   *Something Good* Utah Saints
8   *Friday I'm In Love* The Cure
9   *The Days Of Pearly Spencer* Marc Almond
10 *Bell Bottomed Tear* The Beautiful South
11 *Thunder* Prince & The New Power Generation
12 *Even Better Than The Real Thing* U2
13 *L.S.I.* The Shamen
14 *Disappointed* Electronic
15 *I Don't Care* Shakespears Sister
16 *Do Re Me So Far So Good* Carter USM
17 *Everything About You* Ugly Kid Joe
18 *On A Ragga Tip* SL2
19 *Blue Room* The Orb

CD2

1   *Hazard* Richard Marx
2   *The One* Elton John
3   *I Drove All Night* Roy Orbison
4   *Ain't No Doubt* Jimmy Nail
5   *Unchain My Heart* Joe Cocker
6   *You're All That Matters To Me* Curtis Stigers
7   *You Won't See Me Cry* Wilson Phillips
8   *Four Seasons In One Day* Crowded House
9   *Why* Annie Lennox
10 *Don't Let The Sun Go Down On Me* George Michael and Elton John
11 *One Shining Moment* Diana Ross
12 *Save The Best For Last* Vanessa Williams
13 *My Lovin' (You're Never Gonna Get It)* En Vogue
14 *Joy* Soul II Soul
15 *Don't You Worry 'Bout A Thing* Incognito

▶**Nick Berry**'s 'Heartbeat' is taken from the long-running TV show of the same name which, in 2000, featured an acting turn from **Gary Barlow** playing a scampish musical vagabond who serenaded the townsfolk with his sensitive ballads while chewing the furniture. By coincidence, **Take That** made their *NOW* debut on this volume, rubbing shoulders with the former *EastEnder* who was making his farewell appearance.

▶Welcome back to Harry '**KC**' Casey, veteran of the very first *NOW* alongside **The Sunshine Band** ('Give It Up') and back here via the **KWS** chart-topping cover version of 'Please Don't Go'. On its original release, 'Please Don't Go' was the first US No.1 of the '80s; in the UK it reached No.3.

RELEASED 16 NOVEMBER 1992

HELLO
K.D. LANG

GOODBYE
INXS

▶ Walthamstow, north-east London: home to the dog track featured on the sleeve of **Blur**'s *Parklife* album, to **More Fire Crew** (*NOW 51*), and also to the postcode and band **East 17**, who made their debut here and would go on to appear ten times in all. 'House Of Love', 'Deep' (*NOW 24*), 'West End Girls' (*NOW 25*) and 'It's Alright' (*NOW 27*) all appear on their debut album, entitled. . . *Walthamstow*.

TRACKLISTING NOW 23

CD1

1. *Sleeping Satellite* Tasmin Archer
2. *Just Another Day* Jon Secada
3. *Would I Lie To You?* Charles & Eddie
4. *Shake Your Head* Was (Not Was)
5. *Iron Lion Zion* Bob Marley & The Wailers
6. *Faithful* Go West
7. *Too Funky* George Michael
8. *People Everyday* Arrested Development
9. *For Your Babies* Simply Red
10. *(Take A Little) Piece Of My Heart* Erma Franklin
11. *Too Much Love Will Kill You* Brian May
12. *Alive And Kicking* Simple Minds
13. *Boom Boom* John Lee Hooker
14. *Achy Breaky Heart* Billy Ray Cyrus
15. *Too Much Too Young* Little Angels
16. *Take This Heart* Richard Marx
17. *Jesus He Knows Me* Genesis
18. *Baby Don't Cry* INXS
19. *It's Only Natural* Crowded House

CD2

1. *Who Needs Love Like That* Erasure
2. *Ebeneezer Goode* The Shamen
3. *Run To You* Rage
4. *I'm Gonna Get You* Bizarre Inc feat. Angie Brown
5. *Temptation* Heaven 17
6. *House Of Love* East 17
7. *Don't You Want Me* The Farm
8. *Never Let Her Slip Away* Undercover
9. *Tetris* Dr Spin
10. *Supermarioland* Ambassadors of Funk feat. MC Mario
11. *How Do You Do!* Roxette
12. *Dancing Queen* Abba
13. *A Little Respect* Björn Again
14. *Be My Baby* Vanessa Paradis
15. *Let Me Take You There* Betty Boo
16. *Damn I Wish I Was Your Lover* Sophie B Hawkins
17. *Digging In The Dirt* Peter Gabriel
18. *Book Of Days* Enya
19. *Crying* Roy Orbison & k.d. lang
20. *Barcelona* Freddie Mercury & Montserrat Caballé

▶ **Billy Ray Cyrus** is a one-*NOW* wonder, with 'Achy Breaky Heart' the cause of many an outbreak of frenzied line dancing in 1992. He wasn't finished contributing to popular culture, though: his eldest daughter Destiny Hope, better known as **Miley Cyrus**, has already tripled her father's score from *NOW 76* onwards and looks likely to extend her lead in the future.

▶ To date, Aretha Franklin has not appeared on a numbered *NOW* album, but her sister **Erma** has. Originally recorded in 1967, 'Piece Of My Heart' was later covered by Janis Joplin, Faith Hill and, on *NOW 64*, **Beverley Knight**. **Erma**'s presence on *NOW 23* was prompted by a Levi's TV ad featuring the track, causing the single to make the top ten of the singles chart.

RELEASED 26 APRIL 1993

**HELLO
SHAGGY**

**GOODBYE
SISTER SLEDGE**

▶ A slim entry to the *NOW* series, 'I Feel You' was **Depeche Mode**'s second of only three nods ('Precious' on *NOW 62* would be their last showing to date). However, they are, at the time of writing, the act with the most UK Top 40 hits to their name never to reach No.1. They've hit that chart forty-three times.

CD1

1 *Young At Heart* The Bluebells
2 *Could It Be Magic* Take That
3 *Ain't No Love (Ain't No Use)* Sub Sub feat. Melanie Williams
4 *Exterminate!* Snap!
5 *We Are Family* Sister Sledge
6 *Informer* Snow
7 *Mr Loverman* Shabba Ranks feat. Chevelle Franklin
8 *Oh Carolina* Shaggy
9 *Deep* East 17
10 *Step It Up* Stereo MCs
11 *Tennessee* Arrested Development
12 *Show Me Love* Robin S
13 *Independence* Lulu
14 *The Love I Lost* West End feat. Sybil
15 *No Limit* 2 Unlimited
16 *U Got 2 Know* Cappella
17 *Pressure Us* Sunscreem
18 *Born 2 B.R.E.E.D.* Monie Love
19 *Labour Of Love* Hue And Cry

CD2

1 *Ordinary World* Duran Duran
2 *Love Song For A Vampire* Annie Lennox
3 *Is It Like Today* World Party
4 *Constant Craving* k.d. lang
5 *In Your Care* Tasmin Archer
6 *Looking Through Patient Eyes* PM Dawn
7 *Sweet Harmony* The Beloved
8 *This Time* Dina Carroll
9 *Lady Godiva's Room* Simply Red
10 *Invisible Touch (Live)* Genesis
11 *Are You Gonna Go My Way* Lenny Kravitz
12 *I Feel You* Depeche Mode
13 *Steam* Peter Gabriel
14 *Cats In The Cradle* Ugly Kid Joe
15 *Easy* Faith No More
16 *I Put A Spell On You* Bryan Ferry
17 *Vienna* Ultravox
18 *Hope Of Deliverance* Paul McCartney

▶ **Genesis** – featuring *NOW* club platinum member **Phil Collins** – bid a fond farewell to the series on *NOW 24* with a live version of their 1986 hit (and *NOW 7* entry) 'Invisible Touch'. Ex-band mate **Peter Gabriel** also took one final bow with what was to be not only his last *NOW* appearance, but also his last Top 40 single to date.

'Sweet Harmony' by **The Beloved** remains the London duo's only Top 10 hit single as well as their only *NOW* placing. Earlier hit 'Hello' namechecked **Soul II Soul** alumnus Kym Mayzelle, who appeared on *NOW 18*. It also tips a wink to Cannon & Ball, who did not.

RELEASED 2 AUGUST 1993

HELLO
GABRIELLE

GOODBYE
SHABBA RANKS

▶ 'What's Up?' asked **4 Non Blondes**, and the answer is 78: that many different songs across the *NOW* annals contain the word 'up', from **KC & The Sunshine Band**'s 'Give It Up' on the very first edition to, simply, 'Up' by **Olly Murs feat. Demi Lovato** on *NOW 90*.

TRACKLISTING NOW 25

CD1

1. *Somebody To Love* George Michael & Queen
2. *What's Up?* 4 Non Blondes
3. *I Don't Wanna Fight* Tina Turner
4. *All That She Wants* Ace of Base
5. *Dreams* Gabrielle
6. *You Come From Earth* Lena Fiagbe
7. *Everybody Hurts* R.E.M.
8. *Regret* New Order
9. *Living On My Own* Freddie Mercury
10. *I Will Survive* Gloria Gaynor
11. *Sweat (A La La La La La Long)* Inner Circle
12. *Tease Me* Chaka Demus & Pliers
13. *Shout (It Out)* Louchie Lou & Michie One
14. *Housecall* Shabba Ranks feat. Maxi Priest
15. *Come Undone* Duran Duran
16. *Sunflower* Paul Weller
17. *Ten Years Asleep* Kingmaker

CD2

1. *Tribal Dance* 2 Unlimited
2. *Luv 4 Luv* Robin S
3. *When I'm Good And Ready* Sybil
4. *This Is It* Dannii Minogue
5. *The Ultimate High* The Time Frequency
6. *Do You Really Want Me* Jon Secada
7. *If I Can't Have You* Kim Wilde
8. *West End Girls* East 17
9. *Nothin' My Love Can't Fix* Joey Lawrence
10. *Somewhere* Efua
11. *No Ordinary Love* Sade
12. *This I Swear* Richard Darbyshire
13. *Dream Of Me (Based On Love's Theme)* Orchestral Manoeuvres in the Dark
14. *U R The Best Thing* D:Ream
15. *Caught In The Middle* Juliet Roberts
16. *Break From The Old Routine* Oui 3
17. *I Want You* Utah Saints
18. *Zeroes And Ones* Jesus Jones

▶ A disco revival was in full swing in 1993 and on *NOW 25*: **Gloria Gaynor**'s remixed and reissued 1979 No.1 single 'I Will Survive' (which reached No.5 on its second time around) is the direct recorded link, but there are disco-era cover versions here from **Dannii Minogue** – 'This Is It' charted in 1976 for Melba Moore – and **Kim Wilde**; **Bee Gees** song 'If I Can't Have You' was originally a hit for Yvonne Elliman.

▶ His first band, The Jam, broke up just before the first volume of *NOW* was released, but **Paul Weller** appeared five times between *NOW 3* and *14* as leader of **The Style Council**. There's a certain symmetry to his solo career contributing five appearances to date, with 'Sunflower' being his debut under his own name. 'Have You Made Up Your Mind' on *NOW 70* was his swansong, for *NOW*.

RELEASED 28 MARCH 1994

HELLO
BEE GEES
GOODBYE
RIGHT SAID FRED

▶ Did you find yourself starting to feel hungry reading through the tracklisting at the end of Disc One? Tasty artists **The Cranberries**, **Meat Loaf** and **The Smashing Pumpkins** were chased with a tot of **Gin Blossoms**. **Tori Amos** also brought her 'Cornflake Girl' to the table.

CD1

1. *The Sign* Ace Of Base
2. *Twist And Shout* Chaka Demus & Pliers
3. *Things Can Only Get Better* D:Ream
4. *It's Alright* East 17
5. *Moving On Up* M People
6. *Save Our Love* Eternal
7. *Return To Innocence* Enigma
8. *For Whom The Bell Tolls* The Bee Gees
9. *Come In Out Of The Rain* Wendy Moten
10. *The Perfect Year* Dina Carroll
11. *Everyday* Phil Collins
12. *Now And Forever* Richard Marx
13. *Linger* The Cranberries
14. *Cornflake Girl* Tori Amos
15. *Good As Gold (Stupid As Mud)* The Beautiful South
16. *Rock And Roll Dreams Come Through* Meat Loaf
17. *Rocks* Primal Scream
18. *Hey Jealousy* Gin Blossoms
19. *Disarm* The Smashing Pumpkins

CD2

1. *Doop* Doop
2. *Wonderman* Right Said Fred
3. *Move On Baby* Cappella
4. *Anything* Culture Beat
5. *Let The Beat Control Your Body* 2 Unlimited
6. *I Like To Move It* Reel 2 Real feat. The Mad Stuntman
7. *Come Baby Come* K7
8. *Teenage Sensation* Credit To The Nation
9. *The Way You Work It* EYC
10. *Here I Stand* Bitty McLean
11. *Sweet Lullaby* Deep Forest
12. *Violently Happy* Björk
13. *Uptight* Shara Nelson
14. *Because Of You* Gabrielle
15. *Nervous Breakdown* Carleen Anderson
16. *I Want You* Juliet Roberts
17. *Sail Away* Urban Cookie Collective
18. *Shine On* Degrees of Motion feat. Biti
19. *Lover* Joe Roberts

▶ **Reel 2 Real feat. The Mad Stuntman**'s 'I Like To Move It' had a remarkable afterlife upon dropping away from the chart: in different versions, it has cropped up in multiple *Madagascar* films, and ad campaigns for Chewits (yes, 'I Like To Chew It') and, as 'I Like To Do It', Durex.

▶ The No.1 hit 'Doop' by **Doop** is one of five eponymous *NOW* entries, where artist name and song title are identical. However, we should also doff our caps to **Dee Dee**, **Duran Duran**, **Talk Talk**, **Ting Tings**, **Cash Cash** and **Sub Sub**, all artists where a repetitive naming convention has been no impediment to *NOW* club membership.

RELEASED 1 AUGUST 1994

HELLO
R KELLY

GOODBYE
THE PRETENDERS

▶ 'Sweets For My Sweet' by **CJ Lewis** was originally a UK No.1 hit for The Searchers in 1963. The song was produced by Tony Hatch, who found enormous success with Petula Clark ('Downtown' is one of his) and later still as a TV theme tune composer extraordinaire. 'Emmerdale Farm', 'Neighbours' and 'Mr & Mrs' are all Hatch originals.

TRACKLISTING NOW 28

CD1

1. *Love Is All Around* Wet Wet Wet
2. *I Swear* All-4-One
3. *Don't Turn Around* Ace of Base
4. *Shine* Aswad
5. *(Meet) The Flintstones* B-52s
6. *Crazy For You* Let Loose
7. *U R The Best Thing* D:Ream
8. *Everybody's Talkin'* The Beautiful South
9. *I Believe* Marcella Detroit
10. *I'll Stand By You* The Pretenders
11. *Inside* Stiltskin
12. *Girls And Boys* Blur
13. *Renaissance* M People
14. *Just A Step From Heaven* Eternal
15. *Another Sad Love Song* Toni Braxton
16. *Searching* China Black
17. *You Don't Love Me (No No No)* Dawn Penn
18. *I Wanna Be Your Man* Chaka Demus & Pliers
19. *Always* Erasure
20. *Prayer For The Dying* Seal

CD2

1. *Swamp Thing* The Grid
2. *Everybody Gonfi-Gon* Two Cowboys
3. *Get-A-Way* Maxx
4. *Go On Move* Reel 2 Real feat. The Mad Stuntman
5. *No Good (Start The Dance)* The Prodigy
6. *U & Me* Cappella
7. *Rock My Heart* Haddaway
8. *The Real Thing* 2 Unlimited
9. *Don't Give It Up* Sonic Surfers
10. *What's Up* DJ Miko
11. *Light My Fire* Club House feat. Carl
12. *The Real Thing* Toni Di Bart
13. *Sweets For My Sweet* C J Lewis
14. *Dedicated To The One I Love* Bitty McLean
15. *Whatta Man* Salt 'N' Pepa with En Vogue
16. *Your Body's Callin'* R. Kelly
17. *Dream On Dreamer* Brand New Heavies
18. *Caught In The Middle* Juliet Roberts
19. *Carry Me Home* Gloworm
20. *Absolutely Fabulous* Absolutely Fabulous

▶ **Wet Wet Wet**'s eye-wateringly successful 'Love Is All Around' maintained the top spot from 2 May to 11 September 1994 and was ultimately dislodged by **Whigfield**'s 'Saturday Night' (*NOW 29*). However, its fifteen week run at No.1 kept **All-4-One** and **Let Loose** at No.2 – both are featured here – as well as **Big Mountain**'s 'Baby, I Love Your Way', which would not appear until *NOW 29*.

▶ And talking of the Wet's mega-hit, it was also the first of three No.1s from UK filmmaker Richard Curtis' first three films, this track featured in *Four Weddings and a Funeral*. **Ronan Keating** (*Notting Hill*, *NOW 44*) and **Geri Halliwell** (*Bridget Jones's Diary*, *NOW 49*) complete the trio. 'Jump' by **Girls Aloud** and 'Too Lost In You' by **Sugababes**, both on *NOW 57*, were taken from the 2003 Curtis film, *Love Actually*.

2CD SET

RELEASED 14 NOVEMBER 1994

**HELLO
OASIS

GOODBYE
ROBERT PALMER**

▶ **Louis Armstrong** holds the record as the earliest birth among credited *NOW* performers – he entered this world in 1901 in New Orleans. Sadly, he passed away twenty-three years before being included on *NOW 29*.

TRACKLISTING NOW 29

CD1

1 *Baby Come Back* Pato Banton with Ali & Robin Campbell
2 *Hey Now (Girls Just Wanna Have Fun)* Cyndi Lauper
3 *Baby, I Love Your Way* Big Mountain
4 *Sure* Take That
5 *Sweetness* Michelle Gayle
6 *Saturday Night* Whigfield
7 *Another Night* MC Sar & The Real McCoy
8 *The Rhythm Of The Night* Corona
9 *True Faith* New Order
10 *Right Beside You* Sophie B. Hawkins
11 *7 Seconds* Youssou N'Dour/Neneh Cherry
12 *Stay (I Missed You)* Lisa Loeb And Nine Stories
13 *Mmm Mmm Mmm Mmm* Crash Test Dummies
14 *We Have All The Time In The World* Louis Armstrong
15 *Know By Now* Robert Palmer
16 *What's The Frequency, Kenneth?* R.E.M.
17 *Cigarettes & Alcohol* Oasis
18 *Love Is Strong* The Rolling Stones
19 *Zombie* The Cranberries

CD2

1 *Around The World* East 17
2 *Compliments On Your Kiss* Red Dragon feat. Brian and Tony Gold
3 *Gal Wine* Chaka Demus & Pliers
4 *She's Got That Vibe* R. Kelly
5 *Midnight At The Oasis* Brand New Heavies
6 *Stars* China Black
7 *What's Going On* Music Relief
8 *The Power Of Love* Celine Dion
9 *Confide In Me* Kylie Minogue
10 *Sly* Massive Attack
11 *So Good* Eternal
12 *Some Girls* Ultimate Kaos
13 *Can You Feel It?* Reel 2 Real feat. The Mad Stuntman
14 *Incredible* M Beat feat. General Levy
15 *Trouble* Shampoo
16 *Parklife* Blur feat. Phil Daniels
17 *I Love Saturday* Erasure
18 *When Do I Get To Sing 'My Way'* Sparks
19 *I Want The World* 2wo Third3

▶ Fans of album packaging minutiae will delight in the revelation that *NOW 29* was the first CD set to be sold in the now-familiar 'thin box' format, with both discs fitting inside a case the same size as a standard CD album. Prior to this, double-thickness boxes were used. To clarify this, the top right of the front cover of *NOW 29* carries an explanatory message.

▶ **Music Relief** was a multi-artist charity ensemble raising funds for Rwanda and contained many performers who appeared on *NOW* albums under their own steam, including four-time *NOW* man **Nik Kershaw**; triple inclusions **Paul Young** and **Yazz**; **Aswad, Dannii Minogue** and **Kim Appleby** (two appearances apiece); and **Rozalla** (*NOW 20*), **The Pasadenas** (*NOW 21*), **Angie Brown** (*NOW 23*), **Apache Indian** (*NOW 26*) and **CJ Lewis** (*NOW 28*).

RELEASED 10 APRIL 1995

**HELLO
BOYZONE
GOODBYE
SIMPLE MINDS**

▶ **Nicki French** found fame covering **Bonnie Tyler**'s 'Total Eclipse Of The Heart' on this volume of *NOW*. She would later represent the UK in the 2000 Eurovision Song Contest where – finishing in sixteenth place – she became the lowest-ranking UK entry up to that point. Tyler herself, representing the UK in 2013, trumped this dubious distinction by finishing nineteenth.

CD1

1 *Turn On, Tune In, Cop Out* Freak Power
2 *Whoops Now* Janet Jackson
3 *Love Me For A Reason* Boyzone
4 *Love Can Build A Bridge*
   Cher/Chrissie Hynde/Neneh Cherry
   with Eric Clapton
5 *Stay Another Day* East 17
6 *Over My Shoulder* Mike & The Mechanics
7 *Crocodile Shoes* Jimmy Nail
8 *Independent Love Song* Scarlet
9 *She's A River* Simple Minds
10 *Wake Up Boo!* The Boo Radleys
11 *Tell Me When* The Human League
12 *Sight For Sore Eyes* M People
13 *This Cowboy Song* Sting feat. Pato Banton
14 *Save It 'Til The Mourning After*
   Shut Up & Dance
15 *Bump N' Grind* R. Kelly
16 *Oh Baby I...* Eternal
17 *Protection* Massive Attack feat.
   Tracey Thorn
18 *Glory Box* Portishead
19 *Whatever* Oasis

CD2

1 *Don't Stop (Wiggle Wiggle)*
   The Outhere Brothers
2 *Don't Give Me Your Life* Alex Party
3 *U Sure Do* Strike
4 *The Bomb (These Sounds Fall Into My
   Mind)* Kenny Dope presents The Bucketheads
5 *Push The Feeling On* Nightcrawlers
6 *Always (Something There To Remind Me)*
   Tin Tin Out feat. Espiritu
7 *Baby Baby* Corona
8 *Axel F* Clock
9 *Set You Free* N-Trance
10 *You Belong To Me* JX
11 *Reach Up (Papa's Got A Brand New Pig
   Bag)* Perfecto Allstarz
12 *Cotton Eye Joe* Rednex
13 *Call It Love* Deuce
14 *Here I Go* 2 Unlimited
15 *Run Away* MC Sar & The Real McCoy
16 *Total Eclipse Of The Heart* Nicki French
17 *Suddenly* Sean Maguire
18 *Two Can Play That Game* Bobby Brown
19 *Hoochie Booty* Ultimate Kaos
20 *Bubbling Hot* Pato Banton with Ranking Roger
21 *One* Mica Paris

▶ Ranking Roger, former vocalist from The Beat, joined Birmingham toaster and previous collaborator **Pato Banton** on his 1995 Top 20 hit, 'Bubbling Hot'. On the same volume, Banton himself provides support on **Sting**'s 'This Cowboy Song' while, rounding things off, **The Ordinary Boys** are joined on *NOW 63* by Roger's son, Ranking Junior.

▶ John Reid of **Nightcrawlers** fame – here with their sole *NOW* entry, 'Push The Feeling On' – would later provide **Kelly Clarkson** with her *American Idol* winner's track, 'A Moment Like This'. Simon Cowell repeated the trick when **Leona Lewis** won series three of *The X Factor*, with the single rush-released to become her debut No.1. Leona's version can be found on *NOW 66*.

TAKE THAT

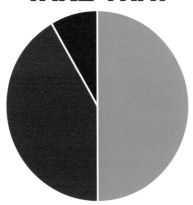

12 appearances
- ■ 3 piece
- ■ 4 piece
- ■ 5 piece

PHIL COLLINS

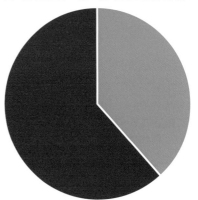

13 appearances
- ■ Happy Phil
- ■ Sad Phil

SUM OF THEIR

KYLIE MINOGUE

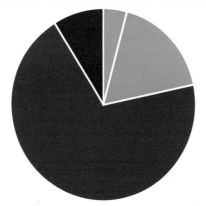

23 appearances
- ■ 1980s
- ■ 1990s
- ■ 2000s
- ■ 2010s

U2

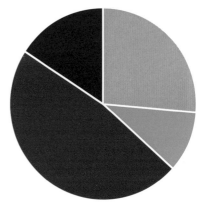

19 appearances
- ■ Earnest Young Men
- ■ Stadium Behemoths
- ■ Irony
- ■ Earnest Old Men

74

ROBBIE WILLIAMS

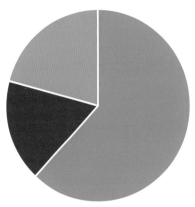

29 appearances
- It's all about Me
- It's about you
- It's about us but mainly Me

OASIS

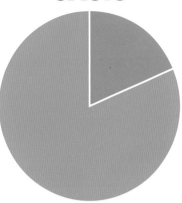

13 appearances
- Noel sings
- Liam sings

PARTS
WHAT MAKES UP THE CAREERS OF OUR BIGGEST *NOW* ARTISTS?

GEORGE MICHAEL

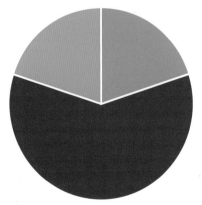

10 appearances
- Stubble
- Beard
- Moustache

SUGABABES

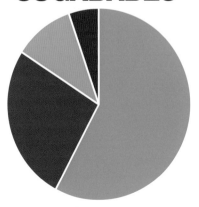

19 appearances
- Mk 2
- Mk 3
- Mk 4
- Mk 5

NB. Sugababes Mk 1 never placed a track on *NOW*.

HOW DO YOU

THE WAY WE LISTEN TO MUSIC HAS CHANGE

 1983

 **AVAILABLE ON** **VINYL LP**

 AVAILABLE ON **CASSETTE**

TAKE YOURS?

RAMATICALLY SINCE THE FIRST *NOW*

2015

AVAILABLE ON

COMPACT DISC

AVAILABLE ON

MINIDISC

AVAILABLE ON

 ## MP3

RELEASED 31 JULY 1995

HELLO
SUPERGRASS
GOODBYE
DURAN DURAN

▶ **Wet Wet Wet**, who headed the tracklisting here, were Track One on three separate *NOW*s – that's a feat that is only beaten by **Queen** (seven times) and matched by **Britney Spears**, **Duran Duran** and **Spice Girls**.

CD1

1. *Don't Want To Forgive Me Now* Wet Wet Wet
2. *A Girl Like You* Edwyn Collins
3. *Common People* Pulp
4. *Alright* Supergrass
5. *In The Summertime* Shaggy feat. Rayvon
6. *Here Comes The Hotstepper* Ini Kamoze
7. *3 Is Family* Dana Dawson
8. *Right In The Night (Fall In Love With Music)* Jam & Spoon feat. Plavka
9. *Hold My Body Tight* East 17
10. *Key To My Life* Boyzone
11. *Kiss From A Rose* Seal
12. *Days* Kirsty MacColl
13. *One Man In My Heart* The Human League
14. *Sour Times* Portishead
15. *Some Might Say* Oasis
16. *Buddy Holly* Weezer
17. *Roll To Me* Del Amitri
18. *I'm A Believer* EMF with Reeves & Mortimer
19. *White Lines (Don't Do It)* Duran Duran feat. Melle Mel & Grandmaster Flash & The Furious Five
20. *Hurts So Good* Jimmy Somerville

CD2

1. *Boom Boom Boom* The Outhere Brothers
2. *I've Got A Little Something For You* MN8
3. *This Is How We Do It* Montell Jordan
4. *Shoot Me With Your Love* D:Ream
5. *I Need Your Loving (Everybody's Got To Learn Sometime)* Baby D
6. *Keep Warm* Jinny
7. *Dreamer* Livin' Joy
8. *Think Of You* Whigfield
9. *Whoomph! (There It Is)* Clock
10. *Humpin' Around* Bobby Brown
11. *Stuck On U* PJ & Duncan
12. *Love City Groove* Love City Groove
13. *Swing Low Sweet Chariot* Ladysmith Black Mambazo feat. China Black
14. *Love Enuff* Soul II Soul
15. *Get Your Hands Off My Man* Junior Vasquez
16. *Freedom* Shiva
17. *Your Loving Arms* Billie Ray Martin
18. *I Need You* Deuce
19. *Son Of A Gun* JX
20. *Only Me* Hyperlogic

▶ Having made their *NOW* debut two editions earlier with 'Cigarettes & Alcohol', **Oasis**'s inclusion here, 'Some Might Say', gave the bothersome Mancunian brotherly band their first UK No.1 hit. They ended up on *NOW*s thirteen times, with their last bow being 'The Importance Of Being Idle' on *NOW 62*. Neither Noel Gallagher's High Flying Birds, nor Liam's post-Oasis band, Beady Eye, have made it in as yet.

▶ Mancunian techno outfit **Clock** hold the distinction of having had the most hit singles that were cover versions in the '90s, nine in all – besides *NOW 31*'s rendition of The Tag Team's 'Whoomph! There It Is', there were also hits for them with 'Axel F' (originally by Harald Faltermeyer and also revived on *NOW 61* by **Crazy Frog**) and *NOW 35*'s 'Oh What A Night', more familiar in its Frankie Valli & The Four Seasons version.

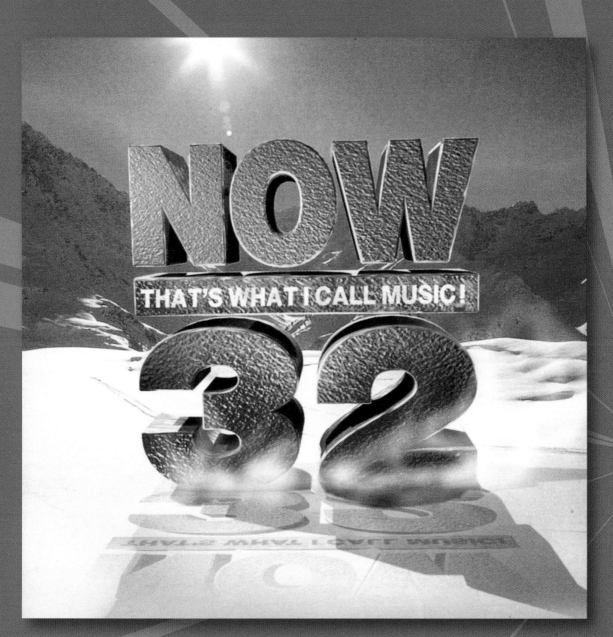

RELEASED 13 NOVEMBER 1995

HELLO
LOUISE

GOODBYE
THE HUMAN LEAGUE

▶ The phrase 'Fee-Fi-Fo-Fum' (**Candy Girls feat. Sweet Pussy Pauline**) is thought to date back to a 1596 poem by Thomas Nash, which in turn was appropriated nine years later by Shakespeare in his play *King Lear*. More commonly associated with the *Jack and the Beanstalk* fairy tale, it first appeared in this form in 1711. Sweet Pussy Pauline therefore completes a long distinguished line of literary giants.

CD1

1. *Heaven For Everyone* Queen
2. *I'd Lie For You (And That's The Truth)* Meat Loaf
3. *Fairground* Simply Red
4. *Hold Me, Thrill Me, Kiss Me, Kill Me* U2
5. *GoldenEye* Tina Turner
6. *Walking In Memphis* Cher
7. *Pretenders To The Throne* The Beautiful South
8. *Light Of My Life* Louise
9. *Big River* Jimmy Nail
10. *Yeha-Noha* Sacred Spirit
11. *Lucky* Radiohead
12. *Sorted For E's & Wizz* Pulp
13. *Country House* Blur
14. *Alright* Cast
15. *Roll With It* Oasis
16. *Yes* McAlmont & Butler
17. *Broken Stones* Paul Weller
18. *I'm Only Sleeping* Suggs
19. *Come Together* The Smokin' Mojo Filters

CD2

1. *Gangsta's Paradise* Coolio feat. LV
2. *Boombastic* Shaggy
3. *Stayin' Alive* N-Trance feat. Ricardo Da Force
4. *I Feel Love* Donna Summer
5. *The Sunshine After The Rain* Berri
6. *Try Me Out* Corona
7. *I Luv U Baby* The Original
8. *Missing* Everything But The Girl
9. *Power Of A Woman* Eternal
10. *I Care* Soul II Soul
11. *La La La Hey Hey* The Outhere Brothers
12. *Big Time* Whigfield
13. *Wrap Me Up* Alex Party
14. *Higher State Of Consciousness* Josh Wink
15. *Renegade Master* Wildchild
16. *Inner City Life* Goldie Presents Metalheads
17. *Don't You Want Me* The Human League
18. *Fee Fi Fo Fum* Candy Girls feat. Sweet Pussy Pauline
19. *I Believe* Happy Clappers
20. *Dreams* Wild Colour
21. *Runaway* E'voke

▶ **Whigfield** is often mistaken for a one-hit wonder but, 'Big Time' was the Danish dance diva's fifth UK Top 40 hit and her only hit single to miss the Top 20. All five singles appeared on her 1995 album, *Whigfield*. The single was a double A-side release coupled with **Wham!**'s 'Last Christmas', which – unchronicled by *NOW* – remains the biggest-selling single never to reach No.1.

▶ **Donna Summer**'s electro pop classic with **Giorgio Moroder**, 'I Feel Love', features here in a re-recorded form. This remains Summer's sole *NOW* entry. Moroder, however, is a veteran of *NOW 4*, with an artist credit alongside **Phil Oakey** on 'Together In Electric Dreams' and the writing and production work on **Limahl**'s 'NeverEnding Story' bearing his name. He also wrote the global smash 'Take My Breath Away' (**Berlin**, *NOW 9*) for the film *Top Gun*.

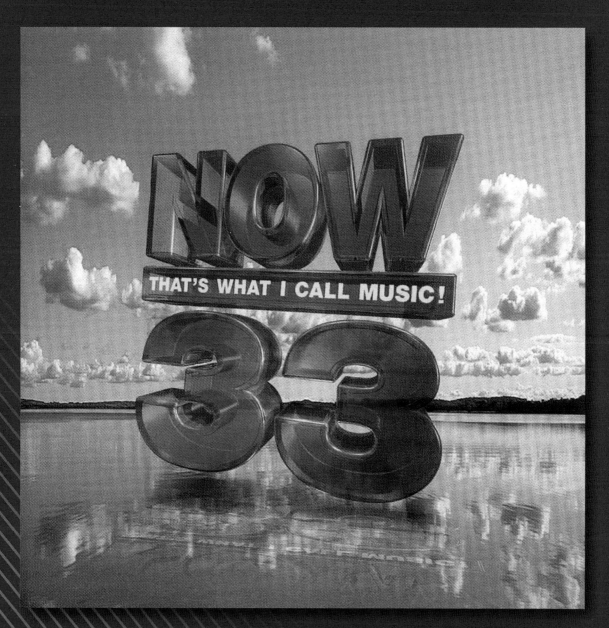

RELEASED 18 MARCH 1996

HELLO
LIGHTHOUSE FAMILY
GOODBYE
THE LEVELLERS

▶ Sheffield's **Prince Naseem** Hamed is the only world featherweight boxing champion to appear on a *NOW*, a title he held from 1995 to 2000. His single with Rochdale rappers **Kaliphz**, 'Walk Like A Champion', was released to commemorate his first successful defence of this title.

CD1

1. *Too Much Love Will Kill You* Queen
2. *Don't Look Back In Anger* Oasis
3. *Spaceman* Babylon Zoo
4. *Going Out* Supergrass
5. *Disco 2000* Pulp
6. *One By One* Cher
7. *Not A Dry Eye In The House* Meat Loaf
8. *Anywhere Is* Enya
9. *'74–'75* The Connells
10. *Father And Son* Boyzone
11. *The Universal* Blur
12. *Out Of The Sinking* Paul Weller
13. *Sandstorm* Cast
14. *All I Need Is A Miracle* Mike + The Mechanics
15. *Fun Fun Fun* Status Quo with The Beach Boys
16. *Perseverance* Terrorvision
17. *Ladykillers* Lush
18. *Just The One* The Levellers
19. *Street Spirit (Fade Out)* Radiohead
20. *Live Forever* Oasis

CD2

1. *Lifted* Lighthouse Family
2. *Good Thing* Eternal
3. *I Just Want To Make Love To You* Etta James
4. *Never Never Love* Simply Red
5. *Give Me A Little More Time* Gabrielle
6. *Thunder* East 17
7. *I Got 5 On It* Luniz
8. *Walk Like A Champion* Kaliphz feat. Prince Naseem
9. *Why You Treat Me So Bad* Shaggy feat. Grand Puba
10. *So Pure* Baby D
11. *Passion* Gat Decor
12. *Disco's Revenge* Gusto
13. *I Need A Lover Tonight* Ken Doh
14. *Beautiful Life* Ace Of Base
15. *In Walked Love* Louise
16. *Not So Manic Now* Dubstar
17. *He's On The Phone* Saint Etienne
18. *Little Britain* Dreadzone
19. *Whole Lotta Love* Goldbug
20. *I Wanna Be A Hippy* Technohead

▶ 'Live Forever' was initially a hit for **Oasis** in August 1994, but eventually appeared on *NOW 33* nineteen months later. Demand for the single remained strong long after its initial chart run and it would go on to spend sixty-six weeks in the Top 100 of the singles chart. All nine singles released by the band up to that point would return to that chart in 1996.

▶ It was farewell here to **Simply Red**, with 'Never Never Love', the ninth of nine *NOW* numbers, *NOW 9* their debut with 'Money's Too Tight To Mention'. The band's *Stars* was the best-selling album in the UK in both 1991 and 1992.

RELEASED 12 AUGUST 1996

HELLO
ROBBIE WILLIAMS

GOODBYE
ORCHESTRAL
MANOEUVRES IN
THE DARK

▶ Despite finishing in eighth place, **Gina G**'s 'Ooh Aah… Just A Little Bit' remains the last UK Eurovision entry to reach No.1 in the UK singles chart. Three other UK entries have also been captured for posterity by *NOW*: **Love City Groove** (*NOW 31*), **Imaani** (*NOW 40*) and **Precious** (*NOW 43*).

CD1

1 *Wannabe* Spice Girls
2 *Freedom* Robbie Williams
3 *Mysterious Girl* Peter Andre feat. Bubbler Ranx
4 *Good Enough* Dodgy
5 *The Day We Caught The Train* Ocean Colour Scene
6 *Theme From 'Mission: Impossible'* Adam Clayton and Larry Mullen
7 *Born Slippy* Underworld
8 *There's Nothing I Won't Do* JX
9 *Ooh Aah... Just A Little Bit* Gina G
10 *Blurred* Pianoman
11 *Don't Stop Movin'* Livin' Joy
12 *Naked* Louise
13 *Return Of The Mack* Mark Morrison
14 *California Love* 2Pac feat. Dr Dre
15 *Groovin'* Pato Banton
16 *Jazz It Up* Reel 2 Real
17 *That Girl* Maxi Priest feat. Shaggy
18 *Macarena* Los Del Mar
19 *Sunshine* Umboza
20 *Higher State Of Consciousness* Wink
21 *Keep On Jumpin'* Todd Terry feat. Martha Wash and Jocelyn Brown
22 *Children* Robert Miles

CD2

1 *Jesus To A Child* George Michael
2 *Wonderwall* Oasis
3 *Slight Return* The Bluetones
4 *Peacock Suit* Paul Weller
5 *Hey God* Bon Jovi
6 *The Only Thing That Looks Good On Me Is You* Bryan Adams
7 *In Too Deep* Belinda Carlisle
8 *Cecilia* Suggs feat. Louchie Lou and Michie One
9 *Charmless Man* Blur
10 *Trash* Suede
11 *One Of Us* Joan Osborne
12 *Instinct* Crowded House
13 *Ocean Drive* Lighthouse Family
14 *On Silent Wings* Tina Turner
15 *Wrong* Everything But The Girl
16 *How Bizarre* OMC
17 *Walking On The Milky Way* Orchestral Manoeuvres In The Dark
18 *Female Of The Species* Space
19 *Walkaway* Cast
20 *Coming Home Now* Boyzone

▶ 'Hey God' by **Bon Jovi** marks the New Jersey quintet's first appearance since 'Livin' On A Prayer' on *NOW 9,* nine years earlier. They had reached the Top 40 on twenty separate occasions in the intervening years and had seen fellow *NOW 9* debutants **Erasure** feature eleven times in their absence.

▶ 'How Bizarre' by **OMC** remains the biggest-selling pop single of all time in frontman Pauly Fuemana's native New Zealand. Fellow countrymen **Crowded House** made their fifth of six *NOW* appearances on this volume. The Finn brothers were awarded an OBE in 1993 for Services to the Music of New Zealand.

RELEASED 18 NOVEMBER 1996

HELLO
SHERYL CROW

GOODBYE
BELINDA CARLISLE

The American band with the second most *NOW* appearances are the **Backstreet Boys**, who opened their account here. Twenty-five per cent of the boys' twelve appearances have concerned one specific internal organ, namely 'I'll Never Break Your Heart', 'Quit Playing Games (With My Heart)' and 'Shape Of My Heart'.

TRACKLISTING NOW 35

CD1

1. *Say You'll Be There* Spice Girls
2. *Fastlove* George Michael
3. *Flava* Peter Andre
4. *If You Ever* East 17 feat. Gabrielle
5. *Breakfast At Tiffany's* Deep Blue Something
6. *Se A Vida E (That's The Way Life Is)* Pet Shop Boys
7. *You're Gorgeous* Babybird
8. *Rotterdam* The Beautiful South
9. *If You're Thinking Of Me* Dodgy
10. *Don't Dream It's Over* Crowded House
11. *Marblehead Johnson* The Bluetones
12. *The Riverboat Song* Ocean Colour Scene
13. *If It Makes You Happy* Sheryl Crow
14. *Milk* Garbage feat. Tricky
15. *Woman* Neneh Cherry
16. *Goodbye Heartbreak* Lighthouse Family
17. *Something Changed* Pulp
18. *Flying* Cast
19. *Beautiful Ones* Suede
20. *Always Breaking My Heart* Belinda Carlisle

CD2

1. *Escaping* Dina Carroll
2. *Words* Boyzone
3. *Someday* Eternal
4. *I'll Never Break Your Heart* Backstreet Boys
5. *Love II Love* Damage
6. *Oh What A Night* Clock
7. *Undivided Love* Louise
8. *When I Fall In Love* Ant & Dec
9. *Don't Make Me Wait* 911
10. *My Love Is For Real* Strike
11. *Insomnia* Faithless
12. *Seven Days And One Week* BBE
13. *I'm Alive* Stretch 'N' Vern
14. *Stamp!* Jeremy Healy And Amos
15. *Follow The Rules* Livin' Joy
16. *Jump To My Beat* Wildchild
17. *Pearl's Girl* Underworld
18. *Neighbourhood* Space
19. *Possibly Maybe* Bjork
20. *Chasing Rainbows* Shed Seven

▶ Meanwhile, on this side of the pond fellow debutants **911** rank fourth among UK all-male vocal groups. Their impressive four-on-the-trot run from *NOW 35* to *38* was with newly written songs – the triple sequence from *NOW 41* to *43* were all cover versions.

▶ Here lay the second of two *NOW* entries for Hounslow's finest, **The Bluetones**. The title 'Marblehead Johnson' does not feature in the song's lyrics and is named in honour of late comedian and satirist Bill Hicks's musical side project. We won't dwell here on the title's provenance, but suffice it to say other Britpop brethren on *NOW 35* were not so quick to embrace such euphemistic sauce.

RELEASED 24 MARCH 1997

HELLO
TEXAS

GOODBYE
EAST 17

▶ Of the **Spice Girls**' ten hit singles from their four-year imperial phase, nine reached No.1 in the UK chart and nine were captured on a *NOW* release across nine consecutive volumes. Only '2 Become 1' is missing. 'Mama' – included here – was a double A-side with 'Who Do You Think You Are', which followed on *NOW 37*.

TRACKLISTING NOW 36

CD1

1. *Mama* Spice Girls
2. *Say What You Want* Texas
3. *Alone* The Bee Gees
4. *Don't Marry Her* The Beautiful South
5. *Don't Speak* No Doubt
6. *Your Woman* White Town
7. *Remember Me* The Blueboy
8. *Virtual Insanity* Jamiroquai
9. *One And One* Robert Miles feat. Maria Nayler
10. *Spinning The Wheel* George Michael
11. *Horny* Mark Morrison
12. *Natural* Peter Andre
13. *Love Guaranteed* Damage
14. *Don't You Love Me* Eternal
15. *Walk On By* Gabrielle
16. *I Can Make You Feel Good* Kavana
17. *Hey Child* East 17
18. *A Different Beat* Boyzone
19. *Anywhere For You* Backstreet Boys
20. *The Day We Find Love* 911

CD2

1. *Discothèque* U2
2. *Breathe* The Prodigy
3. *Block Rockin' Beats* The Chemical Brothers
4. *Nancy Boy* Placebo
5. *What Do You Want From Me?* Monaco
6. *Everyday Is A Winding Road* Sheryl Crow
7. *Beetlebum* Blur
8. *She's A Star* James
9. *Wide Open Space* Mansun
10. *Free Me* Cast
11. *Dark Clouds* Space
12. *Waterloo Sunset* Cathy Dennis
13. *Everybody Knows (Except You)* The Divine Comedy
14. *Indestructible* Alisha's Attic
15. *Shout* Ant & Dec
16. *You Got The Love* The Source feat. Candi Staton
17. *Encore Une Fois* Sash!
18. *Bellissima* DJ Quicksilver
19. *Flash* BBE
20. *Passion* Amen! UK

▶ 'Natural' was the third *NOW* entry for antipodean reality TV star and coffee shop proprietor **Peter Andre**. It was also his third hit single to be written by minor '80s UK soul singer Glen Goldsmith. While the name may not be familiar, Goldsmith had performed on a UK No.1 single as a member of the Band Aid II line up in 1989.

▶ Nothing if not consistent, this is the second of five **Alisha's Attic** singles to make the Top 15 but miss the Top 10. It was the first of two *NOW* placings ('The Incidentals' appears on *NOW 43*). However, one half of the duo, Karen Poole, would feature as a songwriter on future *NOW* entries with songs for **Kylie** ('Red Blooded Women', *NOW 57,* and 'Chocolate', *NOW 58*) and **Sugababes** ('Caught In A Moment', *NOW 59*).

RELEASED 14 JULY 1997

HELLO
THE VERVE
GOODBYE
EN VOGUE

▶ Media mogul, inconvenience enumerator and **Beyoncé** betrother **Jay-Z** started his *NOW* career here, teaming up with **Foxy Brown** on 'I'll Be'. We won't meet Foxy again but Jay's future missus will be among us from *NOW 49* onwards, initially as part of a group.

TRACKLISTING NOW 37

CD1

1. *MMMBop* Hanson
2. *I Wanna Be The Only One* Eternal feat. Bebe Winans
3. *Lovefool* The Cardigans
4. *Just A Girl* No Doubt
5. *Ecuador* Sash! feat. Rodriguez
6. *Where Do You Go* No Mercy
7. *Who Do You Think You Are* Spice Girls
8. *Free* Ultra Naté
9. *Closer Than Close* Rosie Gaines
10. *Star People* George Michael
11. *Don't Let Go (Love)* En Vogue
12. *You Might Need Somebody* Shola Ama
13. *C U When U Get There* Coolio feat. 40 Thevz
14. *Smokin' Me Out* Warren G feat. Ron Isley
15. *I Believe I Can Fly* R. Kelly
16. *Wonderful Tonight* Damage
17. *The Journey* 911
18. *Isn't It A Wonder* Boyzone
19. *Quit Playing Games (With My Heart)* Backstreet Boys
20. *Hey DJ! (Play That Song)* N-Tyce
21. *I'll Be* Foxy Brown feat. Jay-Z

CD2

1. *If I Never See You Again* Wet Wet Wet
2. *Staring At The Sun* U2
3. *Bitter Sweet Symphony* The Verve
4. *Love Is The Law* Seahorses
5. *100 Mile High City* Ocean Colour Scene
6. *Old Before I Die* Robbie Williams
7. *Guiding Star* Cast
8. *Young Boy* Paul McCartney
9. *A Change Would Do You Good* Sheryl Crow
10. *Paranoid Android* Radiohead
11. *Halo* Texas
12. *Sun Hits The Sky* Supergrass
13. *Waltzing Along* James
14. *On Your Own* Blur
15. *Scooby Snacks* Fun Lovin' Criminals
16. *The Saint* Orbital
17. *Nightmare* Brainbug
18. *Ain't Nobody* The Course
19. *Something Goin' On* Todd Terry feat. Martha Wash and Jocelyn Brown
20. *Give Me Love* Diddy

▶ **Shola Ama**, 1998 Brit Award winner for Best British Female Solo Artist, only has two *NOW* showings – twenty-two editions apart – her solo cover of Randy Crawford's 'You Might Need Somebody' featured here.

▶ Admin note: The **Diddy** featured here is not to be confused with P Diddy. *NOW 37*'s Diddy – British DJ born Richard Dearlove – successfully sued the American rap practitioner in 2006 when P Diddy attempted to take the 'P' out of his own stage name.

RELEASED 17 NOVEMBER 1997

HELLO
ALL SAINTS

GOODBYE
ETERNAL

▶ Formed from the remnants of cosmic scouse one-hit wonders **The La's** ('There She Goes', *NOW 18*), **Cast** completed their run of seven consecutive *NOW* appearances on *NOW 38*. This run of hits puts them ahead of all of their Britpop peers in terms of consecutive appearances.

CD1

1 *Tubthumping* Chumbawamba
2 *Spice Up Your Life* Spice Girls
3 *Where's The Love* Hanson
4 *Picture Of You* Boyzone
5 *As Long As You Love Me* Backstreet Boys
6 *Angel Of Mine* Eternal
7 *Raincloud* Lighthouse Family
8 *Got 'Til It's Gone* Janet Jackson
9 *You've Got A Friend* Brand New Heavies
10 *I Know Where It's At* All Saints
11 *Arms Around The World* Louise
12 *Freed From Desire* Gala
13 *Stay* Sash! feat. La Trec
14 *Sunchyme* Dario G
15 *Never Gonna Let You Go* Tina Moore
16 *You Sexy Thing* Hot Chocolate
17 *Da Ya Think I'm Sexy* N-Trance feat. Rod Stewart
18 *Phenomenon* LL Cool J
19 *Party People…Friday Night* 911
20 *Maria* Ricky Martin
21 *Samba De Janeiro* Bellini
22 *Free* DJ Quicksilver

CD2

1 *Yesterday* Wet Wet Wet
2 *You Have Been Loved* George Michael
3 *The Drugs Don't Work* The Verve
4 *Stand By Me* Oasis
5 *All You Good Good People* Embrace
6 *Don't Leave* Faithless
7 *Karma Police* Radiohead
8 *James Bond Theme* Moby
9 *Choose Life* PF Project feat. Ewan McGregor
10 *Lazy Days* Robbie Williams
11 *A Life Less Ordinary* Ash
12 *Black Eyed Boy* Texas
13 *Bitch* Meredith Brooks
14 *Janie, Don't Take Your Love To Town* Jon Bon Jovi
15 *Better Day* Ocean Colour Scene
16 *I'm So Lonely* Cast
17 *Earthbound* Conner Reeves
18 *Lonely* Peter Andre
19 *4 Seasons Of Loneliness* Boyz II Men

▶ It's bad timing and tough luck for Northern trance masters **Dario G**, whose 1997 No.2 hit 'Sunchyme' was kept off the top spot by the biggest-selling single of all time, **Elton John**'s Princess Diana tribute, 'Candle In The Wind 1997'. The Diana single sold 1.5 million copies in its first week, thus creating the biggest-ever sales gap between No.1 and 2. A live version of the original song can be found on *NOW 11*.

▶ The Laurel Canyon connection: **Janet Jackson**'s 'Got 'Til It's Gone' based its refrain on Joni Mitchell's 'Big Yellow Taxi'. The **Brand New Heavies** track which follows Janet on *NOW 38* – 'You've Got A Friend' – is a cover version of the Carole King classic as also recorded by James Taylor, on which Joni Mitchell sings backing vocals.

RELEASED 6 APRIL 1998

HELLO
STEPS
GOODBYE
PULP

▶ Born Eileen Edwards in Ontario, Canada, the artist better known as **Shania Twain** placed four tracks on *NOW* albums from 1998 to 2000 and they were all taken from one album, *Come On Over*. 'You're Still The One' was the first up.

TRACKLISTING NOW 39

CD1

1. *Never Ever* All Saints
2. *High* Lighthouse Family
3. *Together Again* Janet Jackson
4. *Stop* Spice Girls
5. *Torn* Natalie Imbruglia
6. *Kiss The Rain* Billie Myers
7. *Angels* Robbie Williams
8. *Perfect Day* Various Artists
9. *Baby Can I Hold You* Boyzone
10. *Here's Where The Story Ends* Tin Tin Out feat. Shelley Nelson
11. *The Ballad Of Tom Jones* Space with Cerys of Catatonia
12. *Insane* Texas
13. *Weird* Hanson
14. *How Do I Live* LeAnn Rimes
15. *You're Still The One* Shania Twain
16. *Tomorrow Never Dies* Sheryl Crow
17. *No Surprises* Radiohead
18. *Lucky Man* The Verve
19. *This Is Hardcore* Pulp

CD2

1. *Let Me Entertain You* Robbie Williams
2. *Mulder And Scully* Catatonia
3. *Brimful Of Asha (Norman Cook Remix)* Cornershop
4. *It's Like That* Run DMC. vs Jason Nevins
5. *Renegade Master '98* Wildchild
6. *Bamboogie* Bamboo
7. *Found A Cure* Ultra Naté
8. *La Primavera* Sash!
9. *Barbie Girl* Aqua
10. *5,6,7,8* Steps
11. *Let's Go Round Again* Louise
12. *Amnesia* Chumbawamba
13. *Let Me Show You* Camisra
14. *Planet Love* DJ Quicksilver
15. *Treat Infamy* Rest Assured
16. *Prince Igor* Warren G feat. Sissel
17. *Ain't That Just The Way* Lutricia McNeal
18. *Whine And Grine* Prince Buster
19. *The Beat Goes On* The All Seeing I
20. *Believe* Goldie
21. *All I Have To Give* Backstreet Boys
22. *No Way No Way* Vanilla

▶ **Prince Buster**'s 'Whine And Grine' was originally recorded way back in 1968 but owes its appearance in the charts thirty years later, and on this *NOW*, to a TV ad for Levi's jeans. Seven-time *NOW* regulars **Madness** named their band after a Prince Buster song and recorded their debut single, 'The Prince', as a tribute to him.

▶ **Wildchild** (real name Roger McKenzie) first notched a *NOW* placement on edition *32* with 'Renegade Master'. Seven volumes later it was back via a 1998 remix provided by our old friend **Fatboy Slim**, who also revamped **Cornershop**'s 'Brimful Of Asha' to chart success and a place on this tracklisting. Sadly, McKenzie passed away in 1995.

RELEASED 3 AUGUST 1998

HELLO
BILLIE

GOODBYE
CATATONIA

▶ The short but sweet career of Norwegian pop stars **Aqua** is captured four times across the *NOW* series and featured here with their second – of three – UK No.1s, 'Doctor Jones'. Lead vocalist Lene Nystrøm would return fifteen volumes and five years later co-writing **Girls Aloud**'s second hit single, 'No Good Advice'.

CD1

1 *The Grease Megamix* John Travolta And Olivia Newton-John
2 *Viva Forever* Spice Girls
3 *Looking For Love* Karen Ramirez
4 *Because We Want To* Billie
5 *Lady Marmalade* All Saints
6 *Horny* Mousse T. vs Hot 'N' Juicy
7 *Feel It* The Tamperer feat. Maya
8 *Doctor Jones* Aqua
9 *Last Thing On My Mind* Steps
10 *You Make Me Feel Like Dancing* Leo Sayer
11 *Kung Fu Fighting* Bus Stop feat. Carl Douglas
12 *New Kind Of Medicine* Ultra Naté
13 *Stranded* Lutricia McNeal
14 *Lost In Space* Lighthouse Family
15 *All That I Need* Boyzone
16 *Under The Bridge* All Saints
17 *All My Life* K-Ci & JoJo
18 *I Get Lonely* Janet Jackson
19 *Be Careful* Sparkle feat. R. Kelly
20 *Kiss The Girl* Peter Andre

CD2

1 *The Boys Of Summer* Don Henley
2 *Dance The Night Away* The Mavericks
3 *Save Tonight* Eagle Eye Cherry
4 *Road Rage* Catatonia
5 *Big Mistake* Natalie Imbruglia
6 *Come Back To What You Know* Embrace
7 *Sonnet* The Verve
8 *Teardrop* Massive Attack
9 *Legacy* Mansun
10 *Three Lions '98* Baddiel, Skinner and the Lightning Seeds
11 *Vindaloo* Fat Les
12 *The Rockafeller Skank* Fatboy Slim
13 *Needin' U* David Morales presents The Face
14 *I Can't Help Myself* Lucid
15 *Keep On Dancin' (Let's Go)* Perpetual Motion
16 *Everybody Dance (The Horn Song)* Barbara Tucker
17 *Where Are You* Imaani
18 *Night Fever* Adam Garcia
19 *Do You Love Me Boy?* Kerri-Ann
20 *No Tengo Dinero* Los Umbrellos

▶ Distinctive '70s pop chap **Leo Sayer** reached the UK Top 10 with his first seven singles – including the original version of 'You Make Me Feel Like Dancing', a No.2 in 1976. 'Thunder In My Heart' (1977) was the single that broke this run of success, only reaching No.22. However, nearly thirty years later, Sayer would be vindicated when a recording of the track alongside **Meck** reached No.1 and landed a *NOW* entry (*NOW 63*) in the process.

▶ A first for a *NOW* album, with both sides of the double A-sided single appearing – **All Saints'** No.1 'Lady Marmalade'/'Under The Bridge' claimed this distinction. **Patti LaBelle** – who, with her group LaBelle scored the original hit of 'Lady Marmalade' – is a veteran of the series, having appeared on *NOW 7* alongside lead Doobie Brother **Michael McDonald** with 'On My Own'.

RELEASED 23 NOVEMBER 1998

HELLO
VENGABOYS

GOODBYE
LUTRICIA MCNEAL

▶ Irish all-sibling band **The Corrs** appeared only twice on *NOW* albums – their first showing here and then again on *NOW 42*. They are joined in the late '90s *NOW* annals by fellow Irish combo **B*Witched**, who also contain sisters, and by **Boyzone**, featuring the brother of the **B*Witched** Lynches. It's a family affair.

CD1

1 *No Matter What* Boyzone
2 *Millennium* Robbie Williams
3 *Perfect 10* The Beautiful South
4 *Sweetest Thing* U2
5 *I Just Wanna Be Loved* Culture Club
6 *Life Is A Flower* Ace Of Base
7 *Crush* Jennifer Paige
8 *Heartbeat* Steps
9 *Finally Found* Honeyz
10 *Each Time* E-17
11 *Little Bit Of Lovin'* Kele Le Roc
12 *Everything's Gonna Be Alright* Sweetbox
13 *Come Back Darling* UB40
14 *I Want You Back* Melanie B feat. Missy 'Misdemeanor' Elliott
15 *Bootie Call* All Saints
16 *Turn Back Time* Aqua
17 *Too Much* Spice Girls
18 *Someone Loves You Honey* Lutricia McNeal
19 *Question Of Faith* Lighthouse Family
20 *True Colors* Phil Collins
21 *Every Time* Janet Jackson

CD1

1 *Girlfriend* Billie
2 *More Than A Woman* 911
3 *Sex On The Beach* T-Spoon
4 *If You Buy This Record Your Life Will Be Better* The Tamperer feat. Maya
5 *Music Sounds Better With You* Stardust
6 *Up And Down* Vengaboys
7 *Move Mania* Sash! feat. Shannon
8 *Would You...?* Touch and Go
9 *Dreams* The Corrs
10 *My Favourite Game* The Cardigans
11 *Sit Down '98* James
12 *Gangster Trippin'* Fatboy Slim
13 *Falling In Love Again* Eagle Eye Cherry
14 *My Favourite Mistake* Sheryl Crow
15 *No Regrets* Robbie Williams
16 *We Gotta Get Out Of This Place* Space
17 *My Weakness Is None Of Your Business* Embrace
18 *The Incidentals* Alisha's Attic
19 *Relax* Deetah
20 *Home Alone* R. Kelly feat. Keith Murray
21 *Tell Me Ma* Sham Rock

▶ French one-hit wonders **Stardust** contained Thomas Bangalter from **Daft Punk**, who would make their *NOW* debut nine editions later. It would be fourteen years after 'Music Sounds Better With You' that Bangalter and **Daft Punk** partner Guy-Manuel de Homem-Christo would make it to the top of the UK singles chart, with 'Get Lucky'.

▶ It took seven attempts before a solo **Robbie Williams** reached the top spot on the singles chart as he did with 'Millennium'. The track features a re-recording of the string melody from Nancy Sinatra and John Barry's 1967 James Bond theme, 'You Only Live Twice', continuing a Bond association that started on *NOW 5* with **Duran Duran**'s 'A View To A Kill'.

NOW

THAT'S WHAT I CALL MUSIC!

42

RELEASED 29 MARCH 1999

HELLO
STEREOPHONICS
GOODBYE
THE BEAUTIFUL
SOUTH

▶ 'Walk Like A Panther' represents the first of two unlikely comebacks for Sheffield crooner **Tony Christie**. This Top 10 hit written by Jarvis Cocker (whose **Pulp** bowed out on *NOW 39*) would be followed eighteen editions later by a re-release of '(Is This The Way To) Amarillo' in conjunction with Peter Kay and Comic Relief.

CD1

1. *When The Going Gets Tough* Boyzone
2. *Better Best Forgotten* Steps
3. *Believe* Cher
4. *Thank Abba For The Music* Steps, Tina Cousins, Cleopatra, B*Witched & Billie
5. *Goodbye* Spice Girls
6. *End Of The Line* Honeyz
7. *Honey To The Bee* Billie
8. *What Can I Do* The Corrs
9. *Big Big World* Emilia
10. *Killin' Time '99* Tina Cousins
11. *We Like To Party (The Vengabus)* Vengaboys
12. *Witch Doctor* Cartoons
13. *Always Have Always Will* Ace of Base
14. *You Should Be* Blockster
15. *Enjoy Yourself* A+
16. *El Paraiso Rico* Deetah
17. *More Than This* Emmie
18. *Protect Your Mind (For The Love Of A Princess)* DJ Sakin & Friends
19. *Popped* Fool Boona
20. *Colour The World* Sash!
21. *Over You* Justin

CD2

1. *Strong* Robbie Williams
2. *Fly Away* Lenny Kravitz
3. *Praise You* Fatboy Slim
4. *You Don't Know Me* Armand Van Helden/ Duane Harden
5. *Flat Beat* Mr Oizo
6. *Erase/Rewind* The Cardigans
7. *Just Looking* Stereophonics
8. *Walk Like A Panther* The All Seeing I feat. Tony Christie
9. *National Express* The Divine Comedy
10. *Tequila* Terrorvision
11. *How Long's A Tear Take To Dry* The Beautiful South
12. *Wish I Could Fly* Roxette
13. *A Little Bit More* 911
14. *These Are The Times* Dru Hill
15. *My Love* Kele Le Roc
16. *War Of Nerves* All Saints
17. *Inkanyezi Nezazi (The Star and The Wiseman)* Ladysmith Black Mambazo
18. *Tender* Blur
19. *You Don't Have To Say You Love Me* Dusty Springfield

▶ 'Strong' by **Robbie Williams** reached No.4 in the UK singles chart. His next fifteen singles would all reach the Top 10. Former bandmate **Gary Barlow** would release a cheeky/ coincidental riposte six months later, titled 'Stronger' – a No.16 hit unchronicled by *NOW* – which would be his highest charting single until **Take That**'s blockbusting comeback eight years later with 'Patience' (*NOW 66*).

▶ One of the biggest Danish pop bands of all time, **Cartoons** feature here with their single 'Witch Doctor'. The song was originally written in 1958 by Ross Bagdasarian, whose varied career was also notable for a small role in Alfred Hitchcock's *Rear Window* and creating the long-running children's characters Alvin and the Chipmunks.

THE MOST NO.1s
NOW 88

Released in July 2014, *NOW 88* contains the most No.1 singles to date, including a sixth No.1 for *NOW* regular **Calvin Harris**.

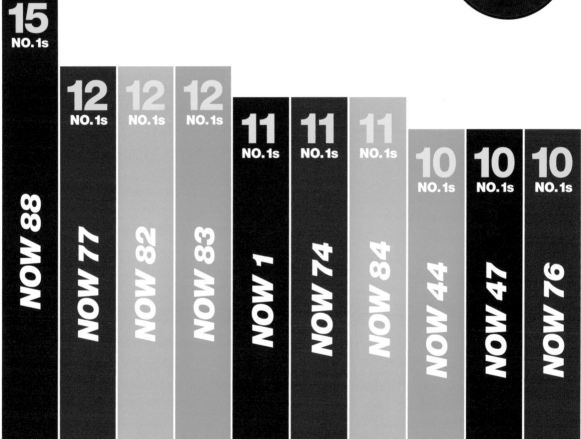

15 NO.1s — NOW 88

12 NO.1s — NOW 77

12 NO.1s — NOW 82

12 NO.1s — NOW 83

11 NO.1s — NOW 1

11 NO.1s — NOW 74

11 NO.1s — NOW 84

10 NO.1s — NOW 44

10 NO.1s — NOW 47

10 NO.1s — NOW 76

MOST NO.1 SINGLES

MOST NO.1 SINGLES?

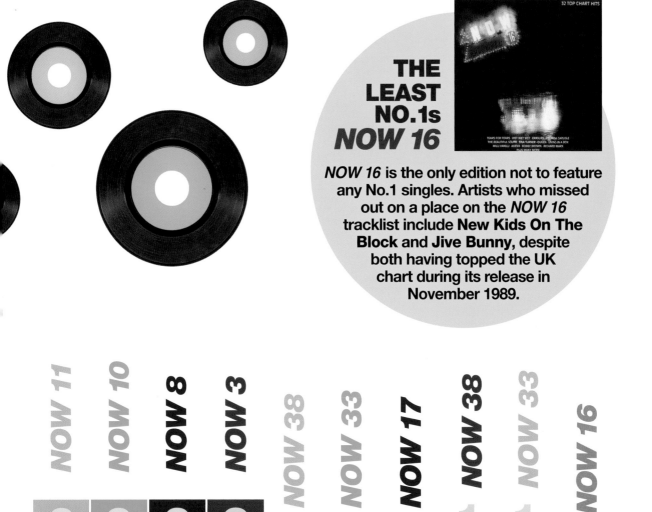

THE LEAST NO.1s
NOW 16

32 TOP CHART HITS

TEARS FOR FEARS · WET WET WET · ERASURE · BELINDA CARLISLE
THE BEAUTIFUL SOUTH · TINA TURNER · QUEEN · LIVING IN A BOX
MILLI VANILLI · ADEVA · BOBBY BROWN · RICHARD MARX
PLUS MANY MORE

NOW 16 is the only edition not to feature any No.1 singles. Artists who missed out on a place on the *NOW 16* tracklist include **New Kids On The Block** and **Jive Bunny**, despite both having topped the UK chart during its release in November 1989.

NOW 11	NOW 10	NOW 8	NOW 3	NOW 38	NOW 33	NOW 17	NOW 38	NOW 33	NOW 16
3 NO.1s	**3** NO.1s	**3** NO.1s	**3** NO.1s	**2** NO.1s	**2** NO.1s	**2** NO.1s	**1** NO.1	**1** NO.1	**0** NO.1s

LEAST NO.1 SINGLES

NEVER APPEARED

Some artists have missed out on canonisation in *NOW* history. We tip a hat to these acts and note their number of Top 75 singles released since 1983.

MADONNA 71

SUPER FURRY ANIMALS 17

RED HOT CHILI PEPPERS 22

BRUCE SPRINGSTEEN 18

METALLICA 19

SHAKIN' STEVENS 19

THE WEDDING PRESENT 17

GREEN DAY 22

ELVIS PRESLEY 40

ONLY APPEARED ONCE

ABBA *NOW 23*

DIDO *NOW 49*

FLEETWOOD MAC *NOW 84*

RICK ASTLEY *NOW 19*

WHITNEY HOUSTON *NOW 74*

CELINE DION *NOW 29*

IRON MAIDEN *NOW 12*

THE SMITHS *NOW 2*

LIONEL RICHIE *NOW 4*

SADE *NOW 25*

WILL SMITH *NOW 61*

Lionel Richie

OUR FAVOURITE
NOW MCs

HAMMER
THE REBEL
SAR
ERIC
NEAT
BONEZ
WILDSKI
MIKEE FREEDOM

MC
Hammer

JOHNNY MARR PLAYS GUITAR

Billy
Bragg
NOW 8

The
Smiths
NOW 2

Banderas
NOW 19

Kirsty
MacColl
NOW 15

Electronic
NOW 22

He may have only one Smiths entry to his name but **JOHNNY MARR** is very much the man that *NOW* alumni turn to in their hour of six-stringed need.

RELEASED 19 JULY 1999

HELLO
GERI HALLIWELL

GOODBYE
MADNESS

▶ Recently reformed reachers **S Club 7** brought some teen pop back to the *NOW* series nine times under this name, including their debut here. Once the septet became a sextet, there were two more to come as, simply, **S Club** – their swansong being the aptly named 'Say Goodbye' on *NOW 55*.

106

CD1

1. *Perfect Moment* **Martine McCutcheon**
2. *You Needed Me* **Boyzone**
3. *I Want It That Way* **Backstreet Boys**
4. *Sweet Like Chocolate* **Shanks & Bigfoot**
5. *Bring It All Back* **S Club 7**
6. *Boom, Boom, Boom, Boom!!* **Vengaboys**
7. *9pm (Till I Come)* **ATB**
8. *Turn Around* **Phats & Small**
9. *Red Alert* **Basement Jaxx**
10. *Without Love* **Dina Carroll**
11. *Look At Me* **Geri Halliwell**
12. *I Breathe Again* **Adam Rickitt**
13. *Viva La Radio* **Lolly**
14. *Doodah* **Cartoons**
15. *Say It Again* **Precious**
16. *Love Of A Lifetime* **Honeyz**
17. *Private Number* **911**
18. *Your Kisses Are Charity* **Culture Club**
19. *Greatest Day* **Beverley Knight**
20. *Word Up* **Melanie G**
21. *Dayz Like That* **Fierce**
22. *Forever* **Tina Cousins**

CD2

1. *Everybody's Free (To Wear Sunscreen)* **Baz Luhrmann**
2. *In Our Lifetime* **Texas**
3. *You Get What You Give* **New Radicals**
4. *Pumping On Your Stereo* **Supergrass**
5. *Lovestruck* **Madness**
6. *Ooh La La* **The Wiseguys**
7. *Hey Boy Hey Girl* **The Chemical Brothers**
8. *Right Here Right Now* **Fatboy Slim**
9. *Saltwater* **Chicane feat. Maire Brennan**
10. *Cloud Number Nine* **Bryan Adams**
11. *Coffee & TV* **Blur**
12. *Beat Mama* **Cast**
13. *Pick A Part That's New* **Stereophonics**
14. *Bring It On* **Gomez**
15. *Secret Smile* **Semisonic**
16. *I Know What I'm Here For* **James**
17. *Synth & Strings* **Yomanda**
18. *Better Off Alone* **DJ Jurgen presents Alice DeeJay**
19. *To Be In Love* **Masters at Work feat. India**

▶ Also back together in 2015 were **Blur**, who bowed out of *NOW* with a spot of 'Coffee & TV'. Lead singer Damon Albarn would return with five-time *NOW* stars **Gorillaz**. Bassist Alex James had already appeared away from **Blur**, with side project **Fat Les** ('Vindaloo') landing on *NOW 40*.

▶ *NOW 43* heralded the arrival of *Eastender*

Martine McCutcheon with her first of five entries from five Top 10 singles. It was a strike rate the envy of fellow soap opera actor **Adam Rickitt** from *Coronation Street*, who landed his sole *NOW* entry and Top 10 single on this edition. Keith Duffy of **Boyzone** and **Shayne Ward** would also eventually prop up the Rovers Return bar.

NOW
THAT'S WHAT I CALL MUSIC!
44

RELEASED 22 NOVEMBER 1999

**HELLO
BRITNEY SPEARS**

**GOODBYE
THE CARDIGANS**

▶ With the first of nineteen entries, US pop diva **Britney Spears** kicks off her *NOW* career in glorious style with '…Baby One More Time'. Having sold in excess of ten million copies around the world, it hit the top spot in every European country in which it was released.

CD1

1 ...*Baby One More Time* Britney Spears
2 *That Don't Impress Me Much* Shania Twain
3 *Mambo No. 5 (A Little Bit Of...)* Lou Bega
4 *Blue (Da Ba Dee)* Eiffel 65
5 *Tragedy* Steps
6 *Mi Chico Latino* Geri Halliwell
7 *She's The One* Robbie Williams
8 *When You Say Nothing At All* Ronan Keating
9 *Northern Star* Melanie C
10 *Kiss Me* Sixpence None the Richer
11 *Summer Son* Texas
12 *Sing It Back* Moloko
13 *Sun Is Shining* Bob Marley vs Funkstar De Luxe
14 *Not Over You Yet* Diana Ross
15 *When The Heartache Is Over* Tina Turner
16 *Canned Heat* Jamiroquai
17 *Burning Down The House* Tom Jones and The Cardigans
18 *Drinking In L.A.* Bran Van 3000
19 *Moving* Supergrass
20 *You'll Be In My Heart* Phil Collins

CD2

1 *If I Could Turn Back The Hands Of Time* R. Kelly
2 *Lift Me Up* Geri Halliwell
3 *What I Am* Tin Tin Out feat. Emma Bunton
4 *I've Got You* Martine McCutcheon
5 *Larger Than Life* Backstreet Boys
6 *Give It To You* Jordan Knight
7 *Sunshine* Gabrielle
8 *Never Let You Down* Honeyz
9 *S Club Party* S Club 7
10 *Mickey* Lolly
11 *2 Times* Ann Lee
12 *We're Going To Ibiza* Vengaboys
13 *Bailamos* Enrique Iglesias
14 *(Mucho Mambo) Sway* Shaft
15 *Don't Stop!* ATB
16 *The Launch* DJ Jean
17 *I See You Baby* Groove Armada feat. Gram'ma Funk
18 *King Of My Castle* Wamdue Project
19 *Back In My Life* Alice DeeJay
20 *Turn It Around* Alena

▶ We bid a very fond farewell to two sixties soul icons on *NOW 44*, whose combined global record sales exceed 300 million. Between them, **Diana Ross** and **Tina Turner** have chalked up seventeen *NOW* appearances, with Turner's stretching way back to the very first volume in 1983 ('Let's Stay Together'). Both of their singles captured here mark their final appearance in the UK Top 10 singles chart.

▶ This edition marks **Tom Jones**'s first appearance since 'Kiss', with **Art of Noise** on *NOW 13*. It is the first of four consecutive *NOW* entries for the leather-lunged coal miner's son from Pontypridd, all duets taken from his No.1 album *Reload*. Tom has never appeared on a *NOW* album by himself.

NOW
THAT'S WHAT I CALL MUSIC!
45

RELEASED 17 APRIL 2000

**HELLO
JAMELIA**

**GOODBYE
AQUA**

▶ 'See Ya'? Quite the opposite. **Atomic Kitten's** first appearance here was to lead to ten more over the next five years – the fourth-highest total for an all-female group. The only kitten to pounce on a *NOW* as a solo artist was **Liz McClarnon** ('Woman In Love', *NOW 63*).

CD1

1. *Rise* Gabrielle
2. *Never Be The Same Again* Melanie C feat. Lisa 'Left Eye' Lopes
3. *Fill Me In* Craig David
4. *Born To Make You Happy* Britney Spears
5. *Show Me The Meaning Of Being Lonely* Backstreet Boys
6. *Sitting Down Here* Lene Martin
7. *Mama Told Me Not To Come* Tom Jones & The Stereophonics
8. *Man I Feel Like A Woman* Shania Twain
9. *Bag It Up* Geri Halliwell
10. *You're My Number One* S Club 7
11. *Cartoon Heroes* Aqua
12. *Shalala Lala* Vengaboys
13. *Ooh Stick You* Daphne & Celeste
14. *See Ya* Atomic Kitten
15. *Don't Call Me Baby* Madison Avenue
16. *Love Me* Martine McCutcheon
17. *Say You'll Be Mine* Steps
18. *Won't Take It Lying Down* Honeyz
19. *Rewind* Precious
20. *Get It On Tonite* Montell Jordan
21. *Sweet Love 2k* Fierce
22. *Every Day I Love You More* Boyzone

CD2

1. *Don't Give Up* Chicane feat. Bryan Adams
2. *Toca's Miracle* Fragma
3. *The Time Is Now* Moloko
4. *Re-Rewind (The Crowd Say Bo Selecta)* Artful Dodger feat. Craig David
5. *A Little Bit Of Luck* DJ Luck & MC Neat
6. *Thong Song* Sisqó
7. *Money* Jamelia feat. Beenie Man
8. *Caught Out There* Kelis
9. *Movin' Too Fast* Artful Dodger feat. Romina Johnson
10. *In Your Arms (Rescue Me)* Nu Generation
11. *Bingo Bango* Basement Jaxx
12. *Killer 2000* ATB
13. *Adelante* Sash!
14. *Merry Christmas Mr Lawrence (Heart Of Asia)* Watergate
15. *Everybody* Progress presents The Boy Wunda
16. *Blow Ya Mind* Lock 'N' Load
17. *Big Girl* Precocious Brats feat. Kevin & Perry
18. *Hammer To The Heart* The Tamperer feat. Maya
19. *Cognoscenti vs Intelligentsia* Cuban Boys
20. *It's Only Us* Robbie Williams
21. *All The Small Things* Blink-182
22. *Natural Blues* Moby
23. *Imagine* John Lennon

▶ **Jamelia feat. Beenie Man** provided the only *NOW* title to be entitled simply 'Money', although currency was also explicitly referred to in the '80s by **Simply Red** (*NOW 5*), **Paul Hardcastle** (*NOW 6*) and **Pet Shop Boys** (*NOW 7*). Recently, only **Sam Smith** has had 'Money On My Mind' (*NOW 87*).

▶ Canadian carouser **Bryan Adams** made his exit here, having debuted all the way back on *NOW 6* in tandem with **Tina Turner** on 'It's Only Love'. Neatly, his last appearance was also in tandem with a *NOW* stalwart: **Chicane**, who have thus far racked up four spots.

RELEASED 24 JULY 2000

HELLO
COLDPLAY

GOODBYE
**FRANKIE GOES TO
HOLLYWOOD**

▶ *NOW 46* marks the beginning of **Kylie Minogue**'s second imperial phase. No.1 'Spinning Around' was her biggest solo hit for six years and all subsequent Top 10 hits to date have been chronicled on a *NOW*. With twenty-three entries, Kylie is ranked third in the list of *NOW* All-Time Greats.

CD1

1. *Oops... I Did It Again* Britney Spears
2. *Reach* S Club 7
3. *It Feels So Good* Sonique
4. *Shackles (Praise You)* Mary Mary
5. *Gotta Tell You* Samantha Mumba
6. *When A Woman* Gabrielle
7. *Spinning Around* Kylie Minogue
8. *Sex Bomb* Tom Jones & Mousse T.
9. *The Bad Touch* Bloodhound Gang
10. *Don't Be Stupid (You Know I Love You)* Shania Twain
11. *Day And Night* Billie Piper
12. *2 Faced* Louise
13. *Try Again* Aaliyah
14. *Bye Bye Bye* *NSYNC
15. *Ghetto Romance* Damage
16. *When I Said Goodbye* Steps
17. *New Beginning* Stephen Gately
18. *The One* Backstreet Boys
19. *Porcelain* Moby
20. *Yellow* Coldplay
21. *A Song For The Lovers* Richard Ashcroft

CD2

1. *You See The Trouble With Me* Black Legend
2. *Groovejet (If This Ain't Love)* Spiller feat. Sophie Ellis-Bextor
3. *Sandstorm* Darude
4. *O.T.B. (On The Beach)* York
5. *I Need Your Lovin' (Like The Sunshine)* Marc Et Claude
6. *The Power Of Love* Frankie Goes To Hollywood
7. *When The World Is Running Down (You Can't Go Wrong)* Different Gear vs The Police
8. *Luvstruck* Southside Spinners
9. *Will I Ever* Alice DeeJay
10. *It's My Turn* Angelic
11. *Airwave* Rank 1
12. *Girls Like Us* B15 Project feat. Crissy D & Lady G
13. *Summer Of Love* Lonyo Comme Ci Comme Ca
14. *Crazy Love* M.J. Cole
15. *Masterblaster 2000* DJ Luck & MC Neat feat. JJ
16. *Freak Like Me* Tru Faith & Dub Conspiracy
17. *Call Me* Jamelia
18. *Uncle John From Jamaica* Vengaboys
19. *Flee Fly Flo* Fe-M@il
20. *For Sure* Scooch
21. *I Want Your Love* Atomic Kitten
22. *Deeper Shade Of Blue* Steps

▶ **Marc Et Claude**'s Germanic techno reading of The Korgis 1980 hit 'Everybody's Got To Learn Sometime' is not the first time a much-altered version of the song has graced *NOW* Towers. On *NOW 31*, **Baby D** followed up their 'Let Me Be Your Fantasy' No.1 with their own re-imagining of The Korgis' track and in doing so landed a Top 3 hit.

▶ It is with a heavy heart that we wave a damp handkerchief in the direction of Holland's departing **Vengaboys** – six consecutive *NOW* appearances spanning *NOW 40* to *46*. In the Great Euro Dance Face Off they concede a tie with Sweden's **Ace of Base**, with six entries apiece. However, they are roundly thrashed by Belgium's **2 Unlimited**, with a truly masterful eight *NOW* placements across ten volumes. Techno! Techno! Techno! Techno!

**HELLO
DAVID GRAY**

**GOODBYE
DARUDE**

▶ **Samantha Mumba**'s 'Body II Body' extensively sampled *NOW 2*, *5* and *7* hero **David Bowie**'s 'Ashes To Ashes'. She hasn't been the only one to draw inspiration from The Dame – **Craig David** uses sections of 'Let's Dance' on 'Hot Stuff' (*NOW 68*) while *NOW 75* features a version of 'Under Pressure' brought to us by the combined might of **Jedward** and **Vanilla Ice**. Bringing things up to date, **Alesso feat. Tove Lo** interpolated 'Heroes' on *NOW 90*.

CD1

1   *Rock DJ* Robbie Williams
2   *Lady (Hear Me Tonight)* Modjo
3   *Life Is A Rollercoaster* Ronan Keating
4   *In Demand* Texas
5   *It's My Life* Bon Jovi
6   *Beautiful Day* U2
7   *Babylon* David Gray
8   *Pure Shores* All Saints
9   *Holler* Spice Girls
10 *Body Groove* Architechs feat. Nana
11 *7 Days* Craig David
12 *Body II Body* Samantha Mumba
13 *Lucky* Britney Spears
14 *Can't Fight The Moonlight* LeAnn Rimes
15 *Natural* S Club 7
16 *It's Gonna Be Me* *NSYNC
17 *I'm Outta Love* Anastacia
18 *You Need Love Like I Do* Tom Jones
    & Heather Small
19 *Kids* Robbie Williams & Kylie Minogue
20 *Trouble* Coldplay

CD2

1   *I'm Over You* Martine McCutcheon
2   *On A Night Like This* Kylie Minogue
3   *Stomp* Steps
4   *Absolutely Everybody* Vanessa Amorosi
5   *Walk Of Life* Billie Piper
6   *Out Of Your Mind* True Steppers and
    Dane Bowers feat. Victoria Beckham
7   *I Turn To You* Melanie C
8   *Silence* Delerium feat. Sarah McLachlan
9   *Sky* Sonique
10 *Kernkraft 400* Zombie Nation
11 *Time To Burn* Storm
12 *Feel The Beat* Darude
13 *Ordinary World* Aurora
14 *You Take My Breath Away* SuReaL
15 *Who The Hell Are You* Madison Avenue
16 *Doom's Night* Azzido Da Bass
17 *Who Let The Dogs Out?* B-Boyz
18 *Country Grammar (Hot...)* Nelly
19 *Unleash The Dragon* Sisqó
20 *Tell Me* Melanie B
21 *Beautiful Inside* Louise
22 *Should I Stay* Gabrielle

▶ **Aurora**'s 'Ordinary World' is the second of four Top 40 hits for the electronic dance group, but their sole *NOW* entry. **Duran Duran**'s 1993 original can be found on *NOW 24*. The group's own *NOW* run had drawn to a close in 1995 after ten appearances across thirty-one volumes; the **Aurora** cover, however, extends the *NOW* career of the Birmingham New Romantics into a third decade.

▶ The teen pop candle burned brilliantly yet briefly at the turn of the century, as witnessed by **Billie Piper**'s eighth (and last) Top 40 single in two years. Chosen as the face of the recently re-launched *Smash Hits*, Piper scored six solo Top 10 hits, one as part of the **Steps, Tina Cousins, Cleopatra, B*Witched** supergroup (*NOW 42*) and three solo No.1 hits – all captured on *NOW*. Her first single, 'Because We Want To' (*NOW 40*), made her – at fifteen – the youngest artist to debut at No.1.

RELEASED 9 APRIL 2001

**HELLO
NELLY FURTADO**

**GOODBYE
MARTINE
MCCUTCHEON**

▶ Say what you like about genial handyman **Bob The Builder** but two singles, both No.1, both chronicled by *NOW* is a pretty decent strike rate ('Mambo No. 5' will appear on *NOW 50*). A month after *NOW 48* was released, the million-selling 'Can We Fix It', written by Paul Joyce, received an Ivor Novello award alongside Pete Townshend, John Barry and **The Clash**, none of whom could renovate a dilapidated barn with quite the same grace and dexterity as Bob.

TRACKLISTING NOW 48

CD1

1 *Whole Again* **Atomic Kitten**
2 *Pure and Simple* **Hear'Say**
3 *Never Had A Dream Come True* **S Club 7**
4 *I'm Like A Bird* **Nelly Furtado**
5 *It Wasn't Me* **Shaggy feat. Ricardo 'Rikrok' Ducent**
6 *Clint Eastwood* **Gorillaz**
7 *Chillin* **Modjo**
8 *I Wanna Be U* **Chocolate Puma**
9 *Everytime You Need Me* **Fragma feat. Maria Rubia**
10 *Always Come Back To Your Love* **Samantha Mumba**
11 *Stronger* **Britney Spears**
12 *It's The Way You Make Me Feel* **Steps**
13 *What Took You So Long?* **Emma Bunton**
14 *The Way You Make Me Feel* **Ronan Keating**
15 *Shape Of My Heart* **Backstreet Boys**
16 *I Need You* **LeAnn Rimes**
17 *Still Be Lovin' You* **Damage**
18 *Paradise* **Kaci**
19 *On The Radio* **Martine McCutcheon**
20 *Please Stay* **Kylie Minogue**
21 *Can We Fix It* **Bob The Builder**

CD2

1 *Somewhere Over The Rainbow* **Eva Cassidy**
2 *Stuck In A Moment You Can't Get Out Of* **U2**
3 *Mr Writer* **Stereophonics**
4 *Don't Panic* **Coldplay**
5 *Inner Smile* **Texas**
6 *Let Love Be Your Energy* **Robbie Williams**
7 *Buck Rogers* **Feeder**
8 *Last Resort* **Papa Roach**
9 *Chase The Sun* **Planet Funk**
10 *Played A Live (The Bongo Song)* **Safri Duo**
11 *Dream To Me* **Dario G**
12 *American Dream* **Jakatta**
13 *I Put A Spell On You* **Sonique**
14 *Feels So Good* **Melanie B**
15 *Case Of The Ex* **Mýa**
16 *Straight Up* **Chanté Moore**
17 *Stutter* **Joe**
18 *Show Me The Money* **Architechs**
19 *Piano Loco* **DJ Luck & MC Neat**
20 *Loco* **Fun Lovin' Criminals**

▶ Cheerio, then, to UK garage artists **DJ Luck & MC Neat** after a zeitgeist-centric three-song *NOW* career. In the DJ bear pit, Luck can hold his own alongside **DJ Quicksilver** and **DJ Sammy** – with three appearances each – but all are left embarrassed by **DJ Fresh**, with six *NOW* entries starting on *NOW 79*. **DJ Mental Theo** (*NOW 69*, alongside **Basshunter**) is still subject to a steward's enquiry for having, frankly, a ridiculous name.

▶ An early appearance here from mighty Norwegian production powerhouse Stargate, the men behind **Samantha Mumba**'s third of six entries. Stargate's first UK hit – 'S Club Party' – appeared on *NOW 44* and following similar success with UK talent – **Blue**, **Billie Piper** – the team would go on to work with some of the biggest global superstars, including **Katy Perry** ('Firework', *NOW 77*), **Rihanna** ('Don't Stop The Music', *NOW 69*) and **Ylvis** ('The Fox – What Does The Fox Say?', *NOW 86*).

RELEASED 30 JULY 2001

HELLO
MIS-TEEQ
GOODBYE
RADIOHEAD

▶ 'All Rise': **Blue** stood to attention for the first time on *NOW 49* and would eventually end up with a total of nine appearances. Between this and *NOW 59* ('Curtain Falls'), they would fail to appear on only *NOW 52* and *55*.

CD1

1. *Eternity* Robbie Williams
2. *Out Of Reach* Gabrielle
3. *Eternal Flame* Atomic Kitten
4. *All Rise* Blue
5. *Don't Stop Movin'* S Club 7
6. *It's Raining Men* Geri Halliwell
7. *Lovin' Each Day* Ronan Keating
8. *Have A Nice Day* Stereophonics
9. *Teenage Dirtbag* Wheatus
10. *The Rock Show* Blink-182
11. *Elevation* U2
12. *Ms Jackson* Outkast
13. *Survivor* Destiny's Child
14. *The Way To Your Love* Hear'Say
15. *More Than That* Backstreet Boys
16. *Don't Let Me Be The Last To Know* Britney Spears
17. *Close To You* Marti Pellow
18. *Thank You* Dido
19. *Destiny* Zero 7
20. *Pyramid Song* Radiohead

CD2

1. *Electric Avenue* Eddy Grant
2. *19-2000* Gorillaz
3. *Do You Really Like It?* DJ Pied Piper and the Masters Of Ceremonies
4. *All I Want* Mis-Teeq
5. *Another Chance* Roger Sanchez
6. *Romeo* Basement Jaxx
7. *Meet Her At The Love Parade 2001* Da Hool
8. *Castles In The Sky* Ian Van Dahl
9. *You Are Alive* Fragma
10. *Here And Now* Steps
11. *Upside Down* A*Teens
12. *Perfect Bliss* Bellefire
13. *I Don't Want A Lover (2001 Mix)* Texas
14. *Never Enough* Boris Dlugosch feat. Róisín Murphy
15. *All For You* Janet Jackson
16. *Who's That Girl?* Eve
17. *Ride Wit Me* Nelly feat. City Spud
18. *Dance For Me* Sisqó
19. *Ring Ring Ring* Aaron Soul
20. *So What If I?* Damage
21. *Lullaby* Melanie B

▶ Another band making their debut here were **Destiny's Child**. While the ladies only appeared twice as a group, **Beyoncé** has clocked up another seven solo showings and **Kelly Rowland**, five. Both would open up their accounts away from **Destiny's Child** on *NOW 54*. Michelle Williams is yet to feature.

▶ One-time-only *NOW* inductees **Bellefire** were a girl band managed by ex-*X Factor* stalwart Louis Walsh. While **Jedward** and **Union J** also made just one visit to a *NOW*, there were more successes over the years for his other band charges, **Boyzone** and **Westlife**. In addition, Walsh oversaw the careers of *NOW* solo artists **Samantha Mumba**, **Ronan Keating** and **Shayne Ward**.

RELEASED 19 NOVEMBER 2001

HELLO
GWEN STEFANI

GOODBYE
LIGHTHOUSE FAMILY

▶ Ironic East Coast rockers **Wheatus** covered **Erasure**'s *NOW 13* classic 'A Little Respect' here, as part of a wave of baggy-shorted pop punkers briefly washing up on *NOW* shores: elsewhere **Alien Ant Farm** covered **Michael Jackson**'s 'Smooth Criminal', while Canada's **Sum 41** and LA's skateboarding reprobates **OPM** also featured.

CD1

1. *Can't Get You Out Of My Head* **Kylie Minogue**
2. *Uptown Girl* **Westlife**
3. *Hey Baby* **DJ Ötzi**
4. *Mambo No. 5* **Bob The Builder**
5. *Chain Reaction* **Steps**
6. *Let's Dance* **Five**
7. *Take Me Home* **Sophie Ellis-Bextor**
8. *Perfect Gentleman* **Wyclef Jean**
9. *What Would You Do?* **City High**
10. *If You Come Back* **Blue**
11. *Turn Off The Light* **Nelly Furtado**
12. *Heaven Is A Halfpipe* **OPM**
13. *Bohemian Like You* **The Dandy Warhols**
14. *Smooth Criminal* **Alien Ant Farm**
15. *Fat Lip* **Sum 41**
16. *A Little Respect* **Wheatus**
17. *Sing* **Travis**
18. *Ain't It Funny* **Jennifer Lopez**
19. *Take My Breath Away* **Emma Bunton**
20. *Don't Need The Sun (To Shine To Make Me Smile)* **Gabrielle**
21. *(I Wish I Knew How It Would Feel To Be) Free – One* **Lighthouse Family**
22. *What If* **Kate Winslet**

CD2

1. *Rapture* **iiO**
2. *Starlight* **Supermen Lovers**
3. *Little L* **Jamiroquai**
4. *Bootylicious* **Destiny's Child**
5. *Purple Hills* **D12**
6. *Let Me Blow Ya Mind* **Eve feat. Gwen Stefani**
7. *I'm A Slave 4 U* **Britney Spears**
8. *One Night Stand* **Mis-Teeq**
9. *Family Affair* **Mary J. Blige**
10. *Baby Come On Over* **Samantha Mumba**
11. *Thinking It Over* **Liberty**
12. *Not Such An Innocent Girl* **Victoria Beckham**
13. *Stuck In The Middle With You* **Louise**
14. *Scream If You Wanna Go Faster* **Geri Halliwell**
15. *Things That Go Bump In The Night* **Allstars**
16. *Set You Free* **N-Trance**
17. *Flawless* **The Ones**
18. *Digital Love* **Daft Punk**
19. *Superstylin'* **Groove Armada**
20. *2 People* **Jean Jacques Smoothie**
21. *21 Seconds* **So Solid Crew**
22. *Because I Got High* **Afroman**

▶ Following her *NOW 46* top pop smash with **Spiller** ('Groovejet'), 'Take Me Home' marked the first solo single proper from **Sophie Ellis-Bextor** and kicked off a run of eight *NOW* entries, all Top 20 singles. The original version of 'Take Me Home' was a US Top 10 hit single for **Cher** as part of her first saunter into disco. Cher's 'Believe' (*NOW 42*) remains one of the biggest-selling singles of all time, with global sales of over 11 million.

▶ **Eminem** has only one solo *NOW* credit to his name – 'Without Me' (*NOW 53*) – but has one additional credit with **Akon** on *NOW 66* ('Smack That'). Marshall Mathers' (uncredited) *NOW* debut here was alongside his Detroit crew, **D12**, on 'Purple Hills'. **Akon** in the meantime is now one of the most highly decorated *NOW* inductees – thirteen entries and counting.

RELEASED 25 MARCH 2002

HELLO
DANIEL BEDINGFIELD
GOODBYE
BACKSTREET BOYS

▶ Trance act **PPK** were the first Russian artists to enter the UK singles chart with 'ResuRection', this event coming a mere forty-seven-and-a-half years after the first chart listings had been published.

CD1

1. *Hero* Enrique Iglesias
2. *Fly By II* Blue
3. *Me Julie* Ali G feat. Shaggy
4. *Gotta Get Thru This* Daniel Bedingfield
5. *More Than A Woman* Aaliyah
6. *Somethin' Stupid* Robbie Williams and Nicole Kidman
7. *The World's Greatest* R. Kelly
8. *Have You Ever* S Club 7
9. *Overprotected* Britney Spears
10. *Murder On The Dancefloor* Sophie Ellis-Bextor
11. *In Your Eyes* Kylie Minogue
12. *Point Of View* DB Boulevard
13. *Something* Lasgo
14. *ResuRection* PPK
15. *The Whistle Song (Blow My Whistle Baby)* DJ Aligator Project
16. *True Love Never Dies* Flip & Fill feat. Kelly Llorenna
17. *Everybody* Hear'Say
18. *The Land Of Make Believe* Allstars
19. *A Mind Of Its Own* Victoria Beckham
20. *Words Are Not Enough* Steps
21. *Calling* Geri Halliwell
22. *I Will Always Love You* Rik Waller

CD2

1. *Handbags and Gladrags* Stereophonics
2. *How You Remind Me* Nickelback
3. *Movies* Alien Ant Farm
4. *In Too Deep* Sum 41
5. *Addicted To Bass* Puretone
6. *Am To PM* Christina Milian
7. *Always On Time* Ja Rule feat. Ashanti
8. *Caramel* City High feat. Eve
9. *Shoulda Woulda Coulda* Beverley Knight
10. *Lately* Samantha Mumba
11. *Drowning* Backstreet Boys
12. *Dance For Me* Mary J. Blige
13. *Crazy Rap* Afroman
14. *Bad Babysitter* Princess Superstar feat. High & Mighty
15. *Oi!* Platinum 45s feat. More Fire Crew
16. *It's Love (Trippin')* Goldtrix presents Andrea Brown
17. *Lazy* X-Press 2 feat. David Byrne
18. *So Lonely* Jakatta
19. *Star Guitar* The Chemical Brothers
20. *Drifting Away* Lange feat. Skye
21. *I Don't Wanna Lose My Way* Dreamcatcher

▶ The highly successful West End and touring musical *The Bodyguard* has a healthy *NOW* pedigree. The role of Rachel Marron in the stage show has been performed by **Beverley Knight** (here on *NOW 51* with her biggest UK hit), **Alexandra Burke** (four *NOW* hits from editions *72* to *81*) and *NOW 54*'s **Zoe Birkett**. In the film that inspired the musical, the role was played by *NOW 74*'s **Whitney Houston**.

▶ **Enrique Iglesias** is the biggest-selling Spanish artist to feature for *NOW* and with eleven entries to his name spanning three decades, he is also one of the most successful male solo stars to appear. In April 2015, UK sales for 'Hero', his breakout No.1 hit from 2002, reached one million copies. 'Hero' was produced by Mark Taylor, who most famously introduced **Cher** to the autotune on her global smash 'Believe' (*NOW 42*).

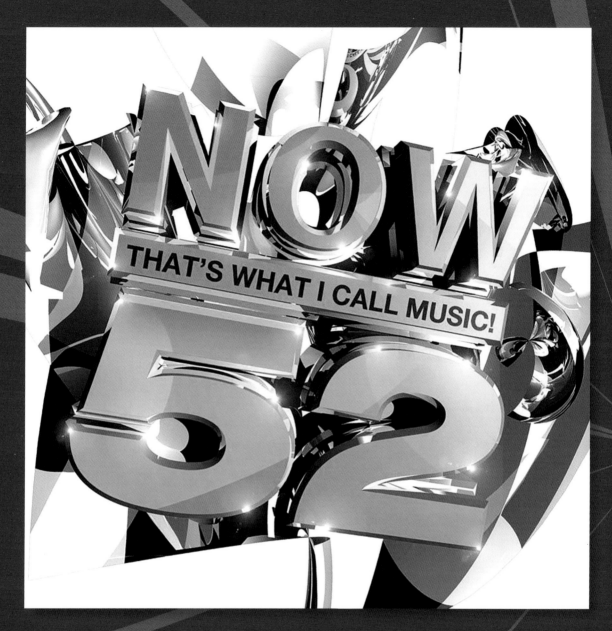

RELEASED 22 JULY 2002

HELLO
MS DYNAMITE

GOODBYE
MOBY

▶ The first of four consecutive appearances for Teutonic techno troublers **Scooter** – a fifth entry would appear on *NOW 70*. 'The Logical Song' – a cover of the 1979 Supertramp soft rock classic – reached No.2 in the UK singles chart, thus beating the original by five places. The Supertramp version was lauded with Ivor Novello awards upon release. The **Scooter** version was not.

CD1

1. *If Tomorrow Never Comes* Ronan Keating
2. *Just A Little* Liberty X
3. *Freeek!* George Michael
4. *Freak Like Me* Sugababes
5. *Love At First Sight* Kylie Minogue
6. *Escape* Enrique Iglesias
7. *Get Over You* Sophie Ellis-Bextor
8. *One Step Closer* S Club Juniors
9. *Follow Da Leader 2002* Nigel & Marvin
10. *The Logical Song* Scooter
11. *Forever* Dee Dee
12. *Shooting Star* Flip & Fill
13. *Be Cool* Paffendorf
14. *Tell It To My Heart* Kelly Llorenna
15. *Shake Ur Body* Shy FX & T-Power feat. Di
16. *It Just Won't Do* Tim Deluxe feat. Sam Obernik
17. *At Night* Shakedown
18. *Dove (I'll Be Loving You)* Moony
19. *Luv Da Sunshine* Intenso Project
20. *(Take Me Away) Into The Night* 4 Strings
21. *Like A Prayer* Mad'House
22. *You* S Club 7

CD2

1. *It's OK!* Atomic Kitten
2. *I'm Not A Girl, Not Yet A Woman* Britney Spears
3. *Foolish* Ashanti
4. *No More Drama* Mary J. Blige
5. *Girlfriend* *NSYNC
6. *When You Look At Me* Christina Milian
7. *Hot In Herre* Nelly feat. Dani Stevenson
8. *It Takes More* Ms Dynamite
9. *Lil' Big Man* Omero Mumba
10. *Rock The Boat* Aaliyah
11. *Freak Mode* The Reelists
12. *My Culture* 1 Giant Leap
13. *Just A Little Girl* Amy Studt
14. *Soak Up The Sun* Sheryl Crow
15. *Pounding* Doves
16. *I Would Die 4 U* The Space Cowboy
17. *American English* Idlewild
18. *Blurry* Puddle of Mudd
19. *We Are All Made Of Stars* Moby
20. *Stop Crying Your Heart Out* Oasis

▶ The hallowed halls of *NOW* are full of multiple entries for the more traditional names – for every Dappy, there are five Pauls. But alongside our ten Davids and eight Johns there remains but one Nigel and a solitary Marvin and therefore, quite naturally, just one **Nigel & Marvin**. The singing siblings are featured here with their sole Top 5 hit 'Follow Da Leader'.

▶ 'Freaks' – or 'Freeeks' if you indulge the unusual spelling employed by **George Michael** – have appeared on a *NOW* release four times, three of those on this one volume. 'Freak Like Me' marks the debut of **Sugababes**, with an eye-watering nineteen *NOW* appearances across twenty-four volumes to follow. However, they were beaten to the punch by **Tru Faith And Dub Conspiracy** on *NOW 46*, with their own 'Freak Like Me'. In both instances, Adina Howard's 1995 single of the same name provided the source of inspiration.

RELEASED 18 NOVEMBER 2002

**HELLO
BUSTED**

**GOODBYE
JANET JACKSON**

▶ **Eva Cassidy**'s cover version of **John Lennon**'s 'Imagine' was not a Top 75 hit single in the UK, however, the album of the same name reached the top of the album charts in 2002. For all her album chart success, Cassidy's Top 40 singles career consists of one chart topper – 'What A Wonderful World', a duet with **Katie Melua** (*NOW 69*) – and nothing else.

CD1

1 *Heaven* DJ Sammy & Yanou feat. Do
2 *Aserejé (The Ketchup Song)* Las Ketchup
3 *Love To See You Cry* Enrique Eglesias
4 *Round Round* Sugababes
5 *The Tide Is High (Get The Feeling)* Atomic Kitten
6 *One Love* Blue
7 *Colourblind* Darius
8 *What I Go To School For* Busted
9 *Got To Have Your Love* Liberty X
10 *It's All Gravy* Romeo feat. Christina Milian
11 *I'm Right Here* Samantha Mumba
12 *What You Got* Abs
13 *I Love Rock 'n' Roll* Britney Spears
14 *Automatic High* S Club Juniors
15 *Come Into My World* Kylie Minogue
16 *My Vision* Jakatta feat. Seal
17 *Music Gets The Best Of Me* Sophie Ellis-Bextor
18 *Heart Of Gold* Kelly Llorenna
19 *Walk On Water* Milk Inc.
20 *Because The Night* Jan Wayne
21 *Pray* Lasgo
22 *Posse* Scooter

CD2

1 *In My Place* Coldplay
2 *Little By Little* Oasis
3 *Electrical Storm* U2
4 *Hero* Chad Kroeger feat. Josey Scott
5 *Check The Meaning* Richard Ashcroft
6 *Imagine* Eva Cassidy
7 *A Thousand Miles* Vanessa Carlton
8 *You Were Right* Badly Drawn Boy
9 *I Love It When We Do* Ronan Keating
10 *Fantasy* Appleton
11 *Dy-Na-Mi-Tee* Ms Dynamite
12 *Feel It Boy* Beenie Man feat. Janet Jackson
13 *James Dean (I Wanna Know)* Daniel Bedingfield
14 *Without Me* Eminem
15 *She Hates Me* Puddle Of Mudd
16 *Girl All The Bad Guys Want* Bowling for Soup
17 *Grace* Supergrass
18 *Jam Side Down* Status Quo
19 *Fascinated* Raven Maize
20 *Shiny Disco Balls* Who Da Funk feat. Jessica Eve
21 *Starry Eyed Surprise* Oakenfold feat. Shifty Shellshock

▶ At 'A Thousand Miles', **Vanessa Carlton**'s introductory hit is the longest distance specified in a *NOW* title. While **The Proclaimers** mentioned that they would walk '500 Miles' twice in the chorus of their hit, the title only mentions that journey once. Bad luck, fellas.

▶ Rock legends Patti Smith and Bruce Springsteen were co-authors of 'Because The Night'. It was originally a Top 5 hit for the Patti Smith Group, becoming their only UK hit single; it would reach the UK chart again in 2002 as covered here by German DJ **Jan Wayne**, and again later still by his Eurodance compatriots **Cascada**. Bruce Springsteen remains a notorious *NOW* no-show.

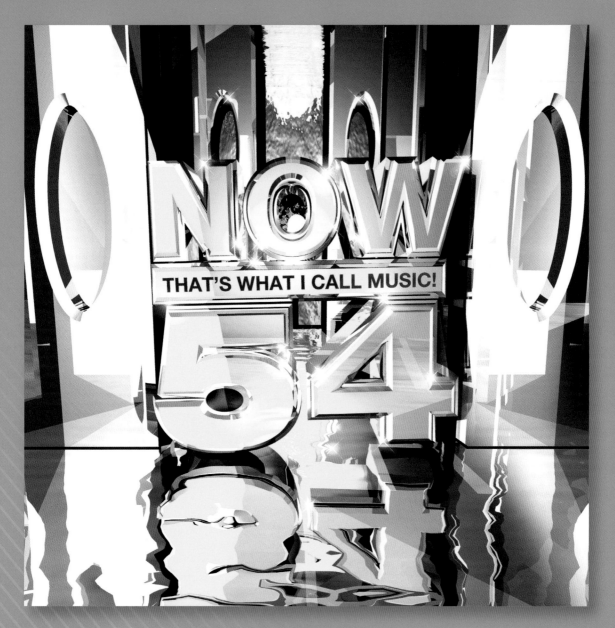

RELEASED 14 APRIL 2003

HELLO
GIRLS ALOUD

GOODBYE
ERASURE

▶ **Kym Marsh** was the only former member of *Popstars* winners **Hear'Say** to register a *NOW* hit as a solo artist, which she did in fact manage twice. This volume of *NOW* features further alumni from that *Popstars* TV series – **Darius** and **Liberty X** – as well as **Girls Aloud** and **One True Voice** from the follow up, *Popstars: The Rivals*.

CD1

1 *All The Things She Said* t.A.T.u.
2 *Like I Love You* Justin Timberlake
3 *Dilemma* Nelly feat. Kelly Rowland
4 *Being Nobody* Richard X vs Liberty X
5 *Make Luv* Room 5 feat. Oliver Cheatham
6 *Move Your Feet* Junior Senior
7 *Sound Of The Underground* Girls Aloud
8 *Year 3000* Busted
9 *Here It Comes Again* Melanie C
10 *I Can't Break Down* Sinéad Quinn
11 *Rushes* Darius
12 *Don't Worry* Appleton
13 *Love Doesn't Have To Hurt* Atomic Kitten
14 *U Make Me Wanna* Blue
15 *'03 Bonnie & Clyde* Jay-Z feat. Beyoncé Knowles
16 *True* Jaimeson feat. Angel Blu
17 *Treat Me Like A Lady* Zoe Birkett
18 *Alive* S Club
19 *Sacred Trust* One True Voice
20 *Cry* Kym Marsh
21 *Keep Me A Secret* Ainslie Henderson

CD2

1 *If You're Not The One* Daniel Bedingfield
2 *Stop Living The Lie* David Sneddon
3 *Feel* Robbie Williams
4 *Songbird* Oasis
5 *Pain Killer* Turin Brakes
6 *Clocks* Coldplay
7 *We've Got Tonight* Ronan Keating & Lulu
8 *Stronger* Sugababes
9 *Street Life* Beenie Man
10 *Hey Ma* Cam'Ron feat. Juelz Santana, Freekey Zeekey, Toya
11 *Work It* Nelly feat. Justin Timberlake
12 *Mundian To Bach Ke* Panjabi MC
13 *Weekend!* Scooter
14 *The Boys Of Summer* DJ Sammy
15 *The Way (Put Your Hand In My Hand)* Divine Inspiration
16 *Flash* Queen & Vanguard
17 *Solsbury Hill* Erasure
18 *Can You Dig It?* The Mock Turtles
19 *Big Yellow Taxi* Counting Crows feat. Vanessa Carlton
20 *Science Of Silence* Richard Ashcroft
21 *Special Cases* Massive Attack

▶ After notching three *NOW*s with *NSYNC, this edition heralds the debut solo appearance from **Justin Timberlake** ('Like I Love You') and in collaboration with **Nelly** ('Work It'). Justin has appeared thirteen times in total to date. Although not the first Justin to grace an edition of *NOW* (that would be, er, **Justin** on *NOW 42*) he is, by some distance, the most highly decorated Justin.

▶ And so we offer a regal salute to dear friends of *NOW*, **Queen**, hanging up the ermine on *NOW 54*. Thirteen appearances since *NOW 2* in 1984, including seven occasions where the band kicked off proceedings, more so than any other artist in *NOW* history. Guitarist **Brian May** would still have one more surprise up his sleeve, however, appearing with an unlikely cohort on *NOW 81*.

NOW SPECIAL EDITIONS

By 1985 *NOW* was established as the premium compilation series in the shops, and highly regarded as a mark of quality. It was a logical move to widen the brief and, starting with *NOW That's What I Call Christmas*, genre-focused albums began to appear.

The following year the first *NOW Summer* was released, and in 1987 a tie-in with *Smash Hits* magazine resulted in an overview of the 1980s up to that point.

Since then there have been numerous iterations of the *NOW Dance* concept, alongside many eras and styles of music that have all been afforded the luxury of a *NOW* volume.

Our round up of the *NOW* special editions concludes with a look at the various DVDs and interactive games that have been released over the last thirteen years.

CHRISTMAS

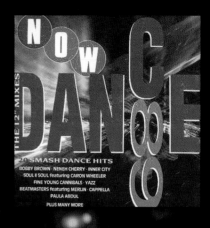

DANCE

Originating as early as 1985, the *NOW Dance* offshoot really got into its stride in the 1990s and early 2000s, averaging more than one volume per year in that period.

NOW SPECIAL EDITIONS

Decades, genres, seasons, countries, weddings: the *NOW* team have turned their attention to all of these over the years.

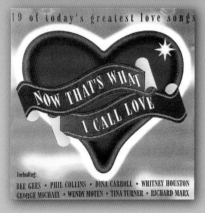

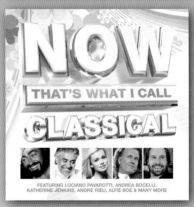

NOW THAT'S WHAT I CALL LOVE

NOW THAT'S WHAT I CALL RUNNING

NOW THAT'S WHAT I CALL BRITAIN

INCLUDING LAND OF HOPE AND GLORY · RULE BRITANNIA · JERUSALEM & I VOW TO THEE MY COUNTRY
FEATURING KATHERINE JENKINS · CLIFF RICHARD · MILITARY WIVES & TOM JONES

NOW THAT'S WHAT I CALL REGGAE

Official Charts Company

NOW THAT'S WHAT I CALL A No.1

Classic Number 1's to celebrate 60 years of the Official Singles Chart

NOW THAT'S WHAT I CALL CHILL

NOW THAT'S WHAT I CALL 90s DANCE

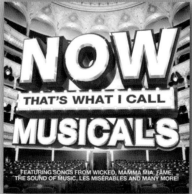

NOW THAT'S WHAT I CALL MUSICALS

FEATURING SONGS FROM WICKED, MAMMA MIA, FAME,
THE SOUND OF MUSIC, LES MISERABLES AND MANY MORE!

NOW THAT'S WHAT I CALL 30 YEARS

RELEASED 21 JULY 2003

**HELLO
MARIAH CAREY**

**GOODBYE
MELANIE C**

▶ Many-headed grime-hydra **So Solid Crew** only graced a *NOW* once – with '21 Seconds' on *NOW 50* – but there was to be further representation from the solo projects of two members of the band. **Romeo** we have seen already ('It's All Gravy' featuring **Christina Milian**, *NOW 53*) and on this edition, **Lisa Maffia** debuted with 'All Over', which for her, in *NOW* terms, it swiftly was.

CD1

1 *Ignition (Remix)* R. Kelly
2 *In Da Club* 50 Cent
3 *Cry Me A River* Justin Timberlake
4 *No Letting Go* Wayne Wonder
5 *Real Things* Javine
6 *Come On Over* Kym Marsh
7 *No Good Advice* Girls Aloud
8 *Not Gonna Get Us* t.A.T.u.
9 *Fool No More* S Club 8
10 *Fast Food Song* Fast Food Rockers
11 *Fly On The Wings Of Love* XTM & DJ Chucky presents Annia
12 *Lately* Lisa Scott-Lee
13 *Shakespeare's (Way With) Words* One True Voice
14 *Husan* Bhangra Knights vs Husan
15 *Loneliness* Tomcraft
16 *Hot In Herre* Tiga feat. Jake Shears
17 *All Over* Lisa Maffia
18 *Satisfaction* Benny Benassi presents The Biz
19 *Deepest Blue* Deepest Blue
20 *Sunlight* DJ Sammy
21 *Damaged* Plummet
22 *Nothing But You* Paul van Dyk feat. Hemstock and Jennings
23 *The Night* Scooter

CD2

1 *Come Undone* Robbie Williams
2 *You Said No* Busted
3 *I Can't Read You* Daniel Bedingfield
4 *Misfit* Amy Studt
5 *Big Sur* The Thrills
6 *God Put A Smile Upon Your Face* Coldplay
7 *Everything Eventually* Appleton
8 *Don't Let Go* David Sneddon
9 *The Long Goodbye* Ronan Keating
10 *Incredible (What I Meant To Say)* Darius
11 *Just The Way I'm Feeling* Feeder
12 *What You Need Is...* Sinéad Quinn
13 *On The Horizon* Melanie C
14 *Free Me* Emma
15 *Say Goodbye* S Club
16 *Shape* Sugababes
17 *Excuse Me Miss* Jay-Z feat. Pharrell Williams
18 *Boy (I Need You)* Mariah Carey feat. Cam'Ron
19 *Mesmerize* Ja Rule feat. Ashanti

▶ A mere three *NOW*s after its first inclusion as recorded by **Nelly**, the song 'Hot In Herre' made a swift return as covered by Canadian electronic artist **Tiga**, assisted by **Jake Shears** on vocals. Shears would return on eight future *NOW* albums in a more familiar guise, as lead singer of **Scissor Sisters**.

▶ Munich-made techno trouper **Tomcraft** only graced the UK Top 40 singles chart the once – with the No.1 hit 'Loneliness' – but the song has proved an enduring one, with six-time *NOW* contributor **Will Young** using the hook line for the chorus of his own 2015 single, 'Love Revolution'.

HELLO
RACHEL STEVENS
GOODBYE
UB40

▶ And so began **will.i.am**'s *NOW* dominance. This was the first of thirteen entries with **The Black Eyed Peas**, with his first solo appearance to follow in seven volumes' time. In total, he has appeared on twenty-eight separate occasions, including twenty-three of the past thirty-four volumes and every year between 2003 and 2014. In short, 31 per cent of *NOW* includes traces of **will.i.am**. #will.i.ammaths

CD1

1. *Where Is The Love?* **The Black Eyed Peas**
2. *Sweet Dreams My LA Ex* **Rachel Stevens**
3. *Slow* **Kylie Minogue**
4. *Guilty* **Blue**
5. *Be Faithful* **Fatman Scoop feat. The Crooklyn Clan**
6. *Crazy In Love* **Beyoncé feat. Jay-Z**
7. *Hole In The Head* **Sugababes**
8. *Jumpin'* **Liberty X**
9. *Superstar* **Jamelia**
10. *Never Leave You (Uh Oooh, Uh Oooh)* **Lumidee**
11. *Stuck* **Stacie Orrico**
12. *Dance (With U)* **Lemar**
13. *Surrender (Your Love)* **Javine**
14. *Maybe* **Emma Bunton**
15. *Sundown* **S Club 8**
16. *Pretty Green Eyes* **Ultrabeat**
17. *Mixed Up World* **Sophie Ellis-Bextor**
18. *Hold On Me* **Phixx**
19. *Invisible* **D-Side**
20. *Pandora's Kiss* **Louise**
21. *Life Got Cold* **Girls Aloud**
22. *If You Come To Me* **Atomic Kitten**

CD2

1. *Are You Ready For Love* **Elton John**
2. *Rock Your Body* **Justin Timberlake**
3. *Something Beautiful* **Robbie Williams**
4. *Someday* **Nickelback**
5. *Sleeping With The Light On* **Busted**
6. *Four Minute Warning* **Mark Owen**
7. *Under The Thumb* **Amy Studt**
8. *Carnival Girl* **Texas feat. Kardinal Offishall**
9. *21 Questions* **50 Cent feat. Nate Dogg**
10. *Rock Wit U (Awww Baby)* **Ashanti**
11. *Pump It Up* **Joe Budden**
12. *Complete* **Jaimeson**
13. *Too Far Gone* **Lisa Scott-Lee**
14. *Love Me Right (Oh Sheila)* **Angel City feat. Lara McAllen**
15. *Finest Dreams* **Richard X feat. Kelis**
16. *Dance With You* **Rishi Rich Project feat. Jay Sean & Juggy D**
17. *Swing Low* **UB40 feat. The United Colours Of Sound**
18. *Silence Is Easy* **Starsailor**
19. *Maybe Tomorrow* **Stereophonics**
20. *Never Gonna Leave Your Side* **Daniel Bedingfield**
21. *Mad World* **Michael Andrews feat. Gary Jules**

▶ Despite fourteen Top 40 hits throughout *NOW*'s active duty, **Tears For Fears** have only appeared once, on *NOW 16* with 'Sowing The Seeds Of Love'. However, a sombre rendering of their debut No.3 hit 'Mad World' by **Gary Jules** and **Michael Andrews** reached No.1 during the festive period, having been re-recorded for the film *Donnie Darko*. Ho Ho Ho.

▶ **Starsailor**'s sole *NOW* credit, 'Silence is Easy', has the unlikely distinction of being one of the last Phil Spector productions released before his enforced 2003 retirement. Spector, however, has appeared before on *NOW* releases with the epic **Righteous Brothers** productions on *NOW 18* and *19* and the re-released 'Imagine' by **John Lennon** on *NOW 45*.

RELEASED 5 APRIL 2004

HELLO
SCISSOR SISTERS

GOODBYE
EMMA BUNTON

It was a *NOW* return after a mere fifty-two editions away for **Kool & The Gang** – while the UK hits had dried up in 1986 for the New Jersey funk and soul collective, **Atomic Kitten** were on hand to revive their 1979 hit 'Ladies Night' and restore them all too briefly to the limelight.

CD1

1 *Toxic* Britney Spears
2 *Milkshake* Kelis
3 *Thank You* Jamelia
4 *Red Blooded Woman* Kylie Minogue
5 *Buleria* David Bisbal
6 *Not In Love* Enrique Iglesias feat. Kelis
7 *Shut Up* The Black Eyed Peas
8 *So Confused* 2 Play feat. Raghav & Jucxi
9 *Dude* Beenie Man feat. Ms Thing and Shawnna
10 *Mysterious Girl* Peter Andre feat. Bubbler Ranx
11 *Cha Cha Slide* DJ Casper
12 *Jump* Girls Aloud
13 *Somebody To Love* Boogie Pimps
14 *Ladies Night* Atomic Kitten feat. Kool & The Gang
15 *I'll Be There* Emma
16 *I Won't Change You* Sophie Ellis-Bextor
17 *Comfortably Numb* Scissor Sisters
18 *Give It Away* Deepest Blue
19 *Take Me To The Clouds Above* LMC vs U2
20 *Come With Me* Special D
21 *Feelin' Fine* Ultrabeat
22 *As The Rush Comes* Motorcycle
23 *Rock Your Body Rock* Ferry Corsten

CD2

1 *Leave Right Now* Will Young
2 *The Closest Thing To Crazy* Katie Melua
3 *Sunrise* Norah Jones
4 *Breathe Easy* Blue
5 *Changes* Kelly Osbourne feat. Ozzy Osbourne
6 *I Miss You* Blink-182
7 *Who's David* Busted
8 *Stacy's Mom* Fountains of Wayne
9 *Take Me Out* Franz Ferdinand
10 *Bring It On* Alistair Griffin
11 *Too Lost In You* Sugababes
12 *Love You Like Mad* VS
13 *Fell In Love With A Boy* Joss Stone
14 *Must Be Love* FYA feat. Smujji
15 *She Wants To Move* N*E*R*D*
16 *Frontin' (Live)* Jamie Cullum
17 *Somewhere Only We Know* Keane
18 *Run* Snow Patrol
19 *Maybe That's What It Takes* Alex Parks
20 *She Believes (In Me)* Ronan Keating
21 *All This Time* Michelle

Keane made their first appearance here with 'Somewhere Only We Know'. Remarkably, the band have notched up five UK albums chart No.1s from five studio releases, an unblemished record which may last forever as the band announced an indefinite hiatus in 2013.

Of the five **Girls Aloud** cover versions to chart, four of the singles can be found peppering the *NOW* canon in both their original version and as recorded by the girls. 'Jump', originally performed by **The Pointer Sisters** on *NOW 4*, is one such instance. The exception is **The Style Council** member Dee. C. Lee's 'See The Day', only captured for *NOW* posterity by **Girls Aloud** on *NOW 63*.

NOW
THAT'S WHAT I CALL MUSIC!
58

RELEASED 26 JULY 2004

HELLO
McFLY

GOODBYE
GEORGE MICHAEL

▶ Louise Gabrielle Bobb – or **Gabrielle** to you and me – delivered thirteen *NOW* entries between *NOW 25* and her final appearance to date on this edition. With six tracks, she appeared on all *NOW*s of 2000 and 2001, excluding *NOW 48* – and she holds the distinction for most *NOW* entries by a UK female solo artist.

CD1

1	*Some Girls* Rachel Stevens
2	*Lola's Theme* The Shapeshifters
3	*Left Outside Alone* Anastacia
4	*Trick Me* Kelis
5	*See It In A Boy's Eyes* Jamelia
6	*F**k It (I Don't Want You Back)* Eamon
7	*F.U.R.B. (F U Right Back)* Frankee
8	*Dip It Low* Christina Milian
9	*Hey Ya!* Outkast
10	*Hey Mama* The Black Eyed Peas
11	*Laura* Scissor Sisters
12	*Flawless (Go To The City)* George Michael
13	*I Like It* Narcotic Thrust
14	*Come As You Are* Beverley Knight
15	*Super Duper Love* Joss Stone
16	*Everybody's Changing* Keane
17	*Matinée* Franz Ferdinand
18	*Golden Touch* Razorlight
19	*In The Shadows* The Rasmus
20	*Now We Are Free* Gladiator feat. Izzy

CD2

1	*Everytime* Britney Spears
2	*Chocolate* Kylie Minogue
3	*The Show* Girls Aloud
4	*5 Colours In Her Hair* McFly
5	*In The Middle* Sugababes
6	*Air Hostess* Busted
7	*Dragostea Din Tei* O-Zone
8	*Bubblin'* Blue
9	*Blood Sweat And Tears* V
10	*It Can't Be Right* 2 Play feat. Raghav & Naila Boss
11	*Move Ya Body* Nina Sky feat. Jabba
12	*It Takes Scoop* Fatman Scoop feat. The Crooklyn Clan
13	*Through The Wire* Kanye West
14	*Maybe* N*E*R*D
15	*1980* Estelle
16	*Eyes On You* Jay Sean feat. The Rishi Rich Project
17	*Call U Sexy* VS
18	*Ride Wit U* Joe
19	*Stay The Same* Gabrielle
20	*Last Thing On My Mind* Ronan Keating feat. LeAnn Rimes
21	*Story Of My Life* Kristian Leontiou
22	*Someone Like Me* Atomic Kitten

▶ While **Outkast** encouraged people to 'shake it like a polaroid picture' on their 2004 global smash 'Hey Ya!', it should be noted that vigorous shaking does nothing in the way of speeding up photo development and may cause the film to separate prematurely and create unseemly blobs on the final picture. Naturally, this didn't stop the Polaroid corporation from exploiting this surprise exposure by cutting a sponsorship deal with Outkast upon the track's release.

▶ Inspiration often comes in the most unlikely of places – as is proved by **Estelle**'s breakout hit '1980', sampling 'Lazy Susan' by '70s US cabaret pop act Dawn & Tony Orlando. Estelle's next *NOW* entry, 'American Boy' (*NOW 70*), would feature **Kanye West**, who coincidentally also starts his first of eleven *NOW* entries to date on this volume.

RELEASED 15 NOVEMBER 2004

HELLO
MAROON 5

GOODBYE
BLUE

▶ British dance act **Eyeopener** had an idiosyncratic approach to deciding which songs to record – their first four singles were 'Open Your Eyes', *NOW 59*'s 'Hungry Eyes', 'Sexy Eyes' and 'Angel Eyes'. You've got to have a system.

CD1

1 *Curtain Falls* Blue
2 *She Will Be Loved* Maroon 5
3 *These Words* Natasha Bedingfield
4 *Radio* Robbie Williams
5 *Thunderbirds Are Go* Busted
6 *Call On Me* Eric Prydz
7 *Love Machine* Girls Aloud
8 *Obviously* McFly
9 *More, More, More* Rachel Stevens
10 *Kinda Love* Darius
11 *Hip To Hip* V
12 *Leave (Get Out)* JoJo
13 *Stolen* Jay Sean
14 *Mary* Scissor Sisters
15 *Bedshaped* Keane
16 *Can't Stand Me Now* The Libertines
17 *The Reason* Hoobastank
18 *Gravity* Embrace
19 *What You're Made Of* Lucie Silvas
20 *I Hope You Dance* Ronan Keating
21 *I Believe My Heart* Duncan James & Keedie

CD2

1 *Nothing Hurts Like Love* Daniel Bedingfield
2 *Stop* Jamelia
3 *Happy People* R. Kelly
4 *My Place* Nelly feat. Jaheim
5 *Let's Get It Started* The Black Eyed Peas
6 *Millionaire* Kelis feat. André 3000
7 *Babycakes* 3 of a Kind
8 *My Neck My Back (Lick It)* Khia
9 *You Can Do It (2004)* Ice Cube feat. Mack 10 and Ms Toi
10 *You Had Me* Joss Stone
11 *Whatever U Want* Christina Milian feat. Joe Budden
12 *Caught In A Moment* Sugababes
13 *You Should Really Know* The Pirates Feat. Enya, Shola Ama, Naila Boss and Ishani
14 *I Like That* Houston feat. Chingy, Nate Dogg & 1-20
15 *Is It 'Cos I'm Cool?* Mousse T. feat. Emma Lanford
16 *Flashdance* Deep Dish
17 *Do You Know (I Go Crazy)* Angel City feat. Lara McAllen
18 *The Weekend* Michael Gray
19 *Get It On* Intenso Project feat. Lisa Scott-Lee
20 *You Won't Forget About Me* Dannii Minogue vs Flower Power
21 *Pump It Up* Danzel
22 *Hungry Eyes* Eyeopener

▶ Modern day market domineers **Maroon 5** opened their *NOW* account here with 'She Will Be Loved', on their way to seven appearances to date. *NOW 80*'s 'Moves Like Jagger', recorded with five-time *NOW* star **Christina Aguilera**, is said to be one of the biggest hits of the download era, with an estimated fourteen million sales worldwide.

▶ A veteran of *NOW 5* ('Icing On The Cake') and vocalist for a pre-fame **Duran Duran**, **Stephen 'Tin Tin' Duffy** would mark his return to the pop firmament by co-writing 'Radio' with **Robbie Williams** as well as his subsequent three *NOW* singles. Neither Duffy's other band The Lilac Time nor 'Hanging Around', a Top 20 hit for Britpop super group and swinging London bon viveurs Me Me Me, have been captured by *NOW*.

RELEASED 21 MARCH 2005

HELLO
AKON

GOODBYE
DARIUS

▶ An end to a momentous era is marked on *NOW 60* through the inclusion of **Geri Halliwell**'s 'Ride It' (or simply, **Geri**, as she is here). After twenty-seven solo appearances and ten for their group the **Spice Girls**, it would be the last entry to date for any member of the illustrious '90s superstars. Geri leads the procession with eight solo entries; **Emma Bunton** close behind on six; **Melanies C** and **B** (and on one occasion **G**) have five apiece, with **Victoria Beckham** rounding off proceedings on three.

TRACKLISTING NOW 60

CD1

1. *What You Waiting For?* Gwen Stefani
2. *Falling Stars* Sunset Strippers
3. *I Believe In You* Kylie Minogue
4. *All About You* McFly
5. *Over And Over* Nelly feat. Tim McGraw
6. *If There's Any Justice* Lemar
7. *I'll Stand By You* Girls Aloud
8. *Out Of Touch* Uniting Nations
9. *Filthy/Gorgeous* Scissor Sisters
10. *Galvanize* The Chemical Brothers feat. Q-Tip
11. *Hush* LL Cool J feat. 7 Aurelius
12. *Only U* Ashanti
13. *Goodies* Ciara feat. Petey Pablo
14. *Locked Up* Akon feat. Styles P.
15. *Spoiled* Joss Stone
16. *Don't Play Nice* Verbalicious
17. *Back To Basics* The Shapeshifters
18. *Ride It* Geri
19. *Shine* The Lovefreekz
20. *Need To Feel Loved* Reflekt feat. Delline Bass
21. *Strings Of Life* Soul Central feat. Kathy Brown
22. *Heartbeatz* Styles & Breeze

CD2

1. *Vertigo* U2
2. *Somebody Told Me* The Killers
3. *Dakota* Stereophonics
4. *This Is The Last Time* Keane
5. *So Here We Are* Bloc Party
6. *Wires* Athlete
7. *Misunderstood* Robbie Williams
8. *Father And Son* Ronan Keating feat. Yusuf Islam
9. *Live Twice* Darius
10. *Wrap My Words Around You* Daniel Bedingfield
11. *Breathe In* Lucie Silvas
12. *Black And White Town* Doves
13. *An Honest Mistake* The Bravery
14. *Do This! Do That!* Freefaller
15. *Thru The Glass* Thirteen Senses
16. *Tumble And Fall* Feeder
17. *Angel Eyes* Raghav feat. Frankey Maxx & Jucxi D
18. *Baby It's You* Jojo
19. *Cradle* Atomic Kitten
20. *Almost Here* Brian McFadden & Delta Goodrem
21. *(Is This The Way To) Amarillo* Tony Christie feat. Peter Kay

▶ 'I'll Stand By You', originally recorded by **The Pretenders** and captured on *NOW 28*, was written by US songwriting duo Kelly and Steinberg. Among their credits, 'True Colours', 'Eternal Flame' and 'I Drove All Night' all appear on a *NOW*, but – like **Girls Aloud** – these all do so as cover versions. 'True Colours' by **Phil Collins** (*NOW 41*) and 'I Drove All Night' by **Roy Orbison** (*NOW 22*) were both originally by **Cyndi Lauper**, and 'Eternal Flame' by **Atomic Kitten** (*NOW 49*) was first recorded by **The Bangles**.

▶ 'Over and Over' by **Nelly** features American superstar Tim McGraw. Country legend McGraw is one of the biggest recording artists in the world, having sold over 40 million albums in the US alone. In 2006, **Taylor Swift** released her debut US single, simply titled 'Tim McGraw'. We will catch up with Taylor on *NOW 72*. McGraw meanwhile remains sat outside *NOW* Towers, face pressed eagerly against the window.

RELEASED 25 JULY 2005

HELLO
JAMES BLUNT

GOODBYE
JOSS STONE

▶ New York rap trio **MVP** (Most Valuable Playas) contained in their ranks Robert Clivillés – who as part of **C&C Music Factory** had been included on *NOW 19* with 'Gonna Make You Sweat (Everybody Dance Now)'. As producers, **C&C Music Factory** had contributed to **Natalie Cole's** 'Pink Cadillac' on *NOW 12*.

TRACKLISTING NOW 61

CD1

1. *You're Beautiful* James Blunt
2. *Ghetto Gospel* 2Pac feat. Elton John
3. *Speed Of Sound* Coldplay
4. *Feel Good Inc.* Gorillaz
5. *Don't Phunk With My Heart* The Black Eyed Peas
6. *Shot You Down* Audio Bullys feat. Nancy Sinatra
7. *They* Jem
8. *Shiver* Natalie Imbruglia
9. *Other Side Of The World* KT Tunstall
10. *Lyla* Oasis
11. *Somewhere Else* Razorlight
12. *I Like The Way* Bodyrockers
13. *Everyday I Love You Less And Less* Kaiser Chiefs
14. *Jerk It Out* Caesars
15. *Smile Like You Mean It* The Killers
16. *Hard To Beat* Hard-Fi
17. *Beverly Hills* Weezer
18. *Lonely No More* Rob Thomas
19. *Forever Lost* The Magic Numbers
20. *Good People* Jack Johnson
21. *Sometimes You Can't Make It On Your Own* U2

CD2

1. *Lonely* Akon
2. *Let Me Love You* Mario
3. *Rich Girl* Gwen Stefani feat. Eve
4. *Switch* Will Smith
5. *Roc Ya Body (Mic Check 1, 2)* MVP
6. *It's Like That* Mariah Carey
7. *N Dey Say* Nelly
8. *Slow Down* Bobby Valentino
9. *Again* Faith Evans
10. *Don't Cha Wanna Ride* Joss Stone
11. *The Avenue* Roll Deep
12. *Crazy Chick* Charlotte Church
13. *So Good* Rachel Stevens
14. *Nasty Girl* Inaya Day
15. *Say Hello* Deep Dish
16. *So Much Love To Give* Freeloaders feat. The Real Thing
17. *Giving You Up* Kylie Minogue
18. *Wake Me Up* Girls Aloud
19. *Axel F* Crazy Frog
20. *Avenues And Alleyways* Tony Christie
21. *You've Got A Friend* McFly
22. *Proud* Heather Small

▶ Arriving among us from the world of ringtones, **Crazy Frog** enjoyed a brief period of time as a bona fide pop star, with **Axel F**, included here, a No.1 hit in the UK. Should you wish to seek out his debut album, *Crazy Frog Presents Crazy Hits*, you will also find frog facsimiles of *NOW 20*'s 'Get Ready For This' (originally by **2 Unlimited**) and 'Whoomph! There It Is' as brought to us on *NOW 31* by **Clock**.

▶ **Elton John** has had UK Top 75 hits duetting with fifteen different acts and three of those collaborations have made it onto *NOW*s – 'Don't Let The Sun Go Down On Me' with **George Michael** (*NOW 22*), here with **2Pac** on 'Ghetto Gospel' and last, but by no means least, 'Tiny Dancer (Hold Me Closer)' with **Ironik feat. Chipmunk** on *NOW 73*. Elton's *NOW* career stretches across seventy editions, having begun on *NOW 4*. Only **Michael Jackson**, who has only featured twice, can claim a greater spread.

NOW THAT'S WHAT I CALL MUSIC! 62

RELEASED 21 NOVEMBER 2005

HELLO
KELLY CLARKSON

GOODBYE
OASIS

With a little bit of assistance from The Animals'
1965 track 'Club-A-GoGo', **Girls Aloud** land their
tenth Top 10 single with 'Biology', a song the
Guardian called the 'best pop single of the last
decade'. 'Biology' was their ninth consecutive
NOW entry and with twenty-one appearances to
date, the girls still hold the record for most
chronicled group across the series.

CD1

1. *Push The Button* Sugababes
2. *Tripping* Robbie Williams
3. *Don't Cha* Pussycat Dolls feat. Busta Rhymes
4. *Bad Day* Daniel Powter
5. *The One I Love* David Gray
6. *Since U Been Gone* Kelly Clarkson
7. *Switch It On* Will Young
8. *Biology* Girls Aloud
9. *I'll Be OK* McFly
10. *I Predict A Riot* Kaiser Chiefs
11. *Do You Want To* Franz Ferdinand
12. *Suddenly I See* KT Tunstall
13. *All About Us* t.A.T.u.
14. *Wake Up* Hilary Duff
15. *I Said Never Again (But Here We Are)* Rachel Stevens
16. *Song 4 Lovers* Liberty X
17. *Baby Goodbye* Friday Hill
18. *Lay Your Hands* Simon Webbe
19. *We Belong Together* Mariah Carey
20. *Electricity* Elton John
21. *Nine Million Bicycles* Katie Melua
22. *You Raise Me Up* Westlife

CD2

1. *DARE* Gorillaz
2. *Hollaback Girl* Gwen Stefani
3. *Diamonds From Sierra Leone* Kanye West
4. *Fix You* Coldplay
5. *The Importance Of Being Idle* Oasis
6. *Don't Lie* The Black Eyed Peas
7. *Can I Have It Like That* Pharrell feat. Gwen Stefani
8. *Ooh La La* Goldfrapp
9. *Doctor Pressure* Mylo vs Miami Sound Machine
10. *Love Generation* Bob Sinclar feat. Gary 'Nesta' Pine
11. *Gasolina* Daddy Yankee
12. *Pon De Replay* Rihanna
13. *1 Thing* Amerie
14. *Belly Dancer (Bananza)* Akon
15. *Big City Life* Mattafix
16. *Welcome To Jamrock* Damian 'Jr Gong' Marley
17. *Precious* Depeche Mode
18. *City Of Blinding Lights* U2
19. *Love Me Like You* The Magic Numbers
20. *Getaway* Texas
21. *Have A Nice Day* Bon Jovi

Gloria Estefan has registered twenty-eight UK Top 40 singles throughout *NOW*'s lifetime, yet this mash up of her own 'Dr Beat' with Scottish electro musician **Mylo**'s 'Drop The Pressure' remains her sole entry in the *NOW* canon. Initially a No.6 hit in 1984, this version beat the original's chart peak by three places.

'Bad Day' by **Daniel Powter** was the Canadian singer-songwriter's sole UK hit and therefore his only *NOW* appearance – but what a hit! A Top 10 single in nineteen countries (including the UK), it was the most played song on European radio in 2005, was the first single to sell two million downloads in the US and to date has sold four-and-a-half-million copies across the world.

NOW
THAT'S WHAT I CALL MUSIC!
63

RELEASED 10 APRIL 2006

HELLO
WILL.I.AM
GOODBYE
TEXAS

▶ **Dead Or Alive**'s 'You Spin Me Round (Like A Record)' was production team **Stock Aitken Waterman**'s first No.1 single in 1985 on its original release. Over twenty years later it was back in the Top 5 and on to a *NOW* album for the first time, the return thanks to a memorable series of appearances on *Celebrity Big Brother* for candid vocalist Pete Burns.

CD1

1 *Put Your Records On* Corinne Bailey Rae
2 *Beep* The Pussycat Dolls feat. will.i.am
3 *My Humps* The Black Eyed Peas
4 *No Tomorrow* Orson
5 *Boys Will Be Boys* The Ordinary Boys
6 *Thunder In My Heart Again*
   Meck feat. Leo Sayer
7 *Say Say Say (Waiting 4 U)* Hi_Tack
8 *You Spin Me Round (Like A Record)*
   Dead Or Alive
9 *It's Chico Time* Chico
10 *That's My Goal* Shayne Ward
11 *Ugly* Sugababes
12 *No Worries* Simon Webbe
13 *All Time Love* Will Young
14 *Because Of You* Kelly Clarkson
15 *Amazing* Westlife
16 *Hang Up* Andy Abraham
17 *I Wanna Hold You* McFly
18 *Ticket Outta Loserville* Son Of Dork
19 *One More Night Alone* Friday Hill
20 *A Night To Remember* Liberty X
21 *If It's Lovin' That You Want* Rihanna
22 *Woman In Love* Liz McClarnon
23 *See The Day* Girls Aloud

CD2

1 *JCB Song* Nizlopi
2 *Nature's Law* Embrace
3 *Advertising Space* Robbie Williams
4 *Talk* Coldplay
5 *Analogue (All I Want)* a-ha
6 *Sewn* The Feeling
7 *Break The Night With Colour*
   Richard Ashcroft
8 *Sleep* Texas
9 *Modern Way* Kaiser Chiefs
10 *All Because Of You* U2
11 *Sugar, We're Goin Down*
   Fall Out Boy
12 *Ride A White Horse* Goldfrapp
13 *Dirty Harry* Gorillaz
14 *Bounce, Shake, Move, Stop!* MVP
15 *I'll Be Ready* Sunblock
16 *Incredible* The Shapeshifters
17 *You Got The Love* The Source
   feat. Candi Staton
18 *Grow* Kubb
19 *Heartbeats* José González

▶ **Blue** boy **Simon Webbe** made the second of three solo showings here – away from the band. **Duncan James** has also featured on a *NOW*, duetting with **Keedie** on edition *59*. Despite each achieving Top 20 solo hits, neither Lee Ryan nor Antony Costa have appeared in the series.

▶ With digital sales yet to contribute to the chart, 'No Tomorrow' by **Orson** claims the unfortunate accolade of 'Lowest Selling No.1 Single of All Time'. A meagre 17,694 copies were sold in its second week at the top.

RELEASED 24 JULY 2006

HELLO
P!NK

GOODBYE
RONAN KEATING

▶ Prior to **Gnarls Barkley**, there had been eleven separate occasions on which a song called 'Crazy' made the UK Top 40 – including two mixes of the same Mark Morrison track. The only previous occasion a 'Crazy' was captured by *NOW* was **Seal**'s No.2 hit in 1990, which can be found on *NOW 19*. The **Gnarls Barkley** track captured here was also the longest-running No.1 single (nine weeks) since **Wet Wet Wet**'s 'Love Is All Around' in 1994 (*NOW 28*).

TRACKLISTING NOW 64

CD1

1. *Crazy* Gnarls Barkley
2. *Maneater* Nelly Furtado
3. *From Paris To Berlin* Infernal
4. *Voodoo Child* Rogue Traders
5. *Don't Stop Me Now* McFly
6. *Who Knew* P!nk
7. *I Wish I Was A Punk Rocker (With Flowers In My Hair)* Sandi Thom
8. *She Moves In Her Own Way* The Kooks
9. *Fill My Little World* The Feeling
10. *Is It Any Wonder?* Keane
11. *You're All I Have* Snow Patrol
12. *In The Morning* Razorlight
13. *Bright Idea* Orson
14. *Valerie* The Zutons
15. *Bang Bang You're Dead* Dirty Pretty Things
16. *Monster* The Automatic
17. *Faster Kill Pussycat* Oakenfold feat. Brittany Murphy
18. *Stoned In Love* Chicane feat. Tom Jones
19. *Country Girl* Primal Scream
20. *Who Says You Can't Go Home* Bon Jovi
21. *Up All Night* Matt Willis
22. *Dance, Dance* Fall Out Boy

CD2

1. *Smile* Lily Allen
2. *SOS* Rihanna
3. *Pump It* The Black Eyed Peas
4. *Buttons* The Pussycat Dolls feat. Snoop Dogg
5. *So Sick* Ne-Yo
6. *Touch It* Busta Rhymes
7. *Say I* Christina Milian feat. Young Jeezy
8. *Mas Que Nada* Sérgio Mendes feat. The Black Eyed Peas
9. *Nine2five* The Ordinary Boys vs Lady Sovereign
10. *Red Dress* Sugababes
11. *Somebody's Watching Me* BeatFreakz
12. *First Time* Sunblock feat. Robin Beck
13. *World, Hold On (Children Of The Sky)* Bob Sinclar feat. Steve Edwards
14. *Tell Me Why* Supermode
15. *Horny As A Dandy* Mousse T. vs The Dandy Warhols
16. *Sensitivity* The Shapeshifters & Chic
17. *Piece Of My Heart* Beverley Knight
18. *You Give Me Something* James Morrison
19. *Who Am I* Will Young
20. *All Over Again* Ronan Keating and Kate Rusby
21. *Whole Lotta History* Girls Aloud

▶ Now widely recognized as an **Amy Winehouse** standard, the original version of 'Valerie' can be found here performed by Liverpool's **The Zutons**, with their sole *NOW* endorsement. Their inclusion pre-dates the **Mark Ronson feat. Amy Winehouse** cover four volumes later. Prior to 2015, it was the highest-charting single for all of the above artists; however, **Mark Ronson**'s globe-straddling mega-hit on *NOW 90* would put paid to that.

▶ When World Cup Fever strikes, Brazilian samba is never far away, even when the host nation is Germany. And so it was in 2006, with **The Black Eyed Peas**-assisted version of **Sergio Mendes**'s evergreen 'Mas Que Nada' a No.6 hit in the UK, which also contained a sample from the band's 'Hey Mama' (*NOW 58*). Often mistranslated, the original Brazilian Portuguese meaning of the phrase 'Mas Que Nada' translates, using the popular youth parlance of the day, as 'whatever'.

CRAIG DAVID'S DIARY
NOVEMBER 2000

Monday
Met this girl

Tuesday
Took her for a drink

Wednesday
Making love

Thursday
Making love

Friday
Making love

Saturday
Making love

Sunday
Chilled

Craig David, 'Seven Days',
NOW 47

THE WORLD REVOLVES AROUND
NENEH CHERRY

Unfinished Sympathy
MASSIVE ATTACK
NOW 19

Produced by Johnny Dollar

Rise
GABRIELLE
NOW 45

Co-Written by Robert Del Naja

**Manchild
NENEH CHERRY**
NOW 15

Produced by Cameron McVey

Never Ever
ALL SAINTS
NOW 39

Co-writer

Beat Dis
BOMB THE BASS
NOW 11

Produced by Tim Simenon

Buffalo Stance
NENEH CHERRY
NOW 14

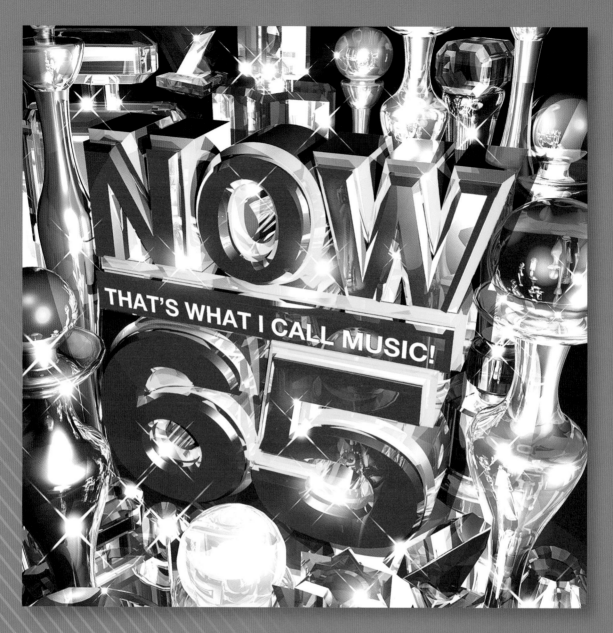

RELEASED 20 NOVEMBER 2006

HELLO
AMY WINEHOUSE

GOODBYE
ALL SAINTS

▶ The last song to be played in full on the original weekly run of *Top of the Pops* was **Shakira feat. Wyclef Jean**'s 'Hips Don't Lie', which was No.1 when the show ended on 30 July 2006. The last act to perform a song in the studio (as opposed to on video) on the long-running programme was **Snow Patrol** with 'Chasing Cars' – also captured on this *NOW*.

TRACKLISTING NOW 65

CD1

1. *I Don't Feel Like Dancin'* **Scissor Sisters**
2. *Hips Don't Lie* **Shakira feat. Wyclef Jean**
3. *Something Kinda Ooooh* **Girls Aloud**
4. *Chelsea Dagger* **The Fratellis**
5. *Rehab* **Amy Winehouse**
6. *Wonderful World* **James Morrison**
7. *Lovelight* **Robbie Williams**
8. *Ain't No Other Man* **Christina Aguilera**
9. *SexyBack* **Justin Timberlake**
10. *Promiscuous* **Nelly Furtado feat. Timbaland**
11. *Déja Vu* **Beyoncé**
12. *Ridin'* **Chamillionaire feat. Krayzie Bone**
13. *Rock This Party (Everybody Dance Now)* **Bob Sinclar & Cutee B feat. Dollarman & Big Ali & Makedah**
14. *Put Your Hands Up For Detroit* **Fedde Le Grand**
15. *London Bridge* **Fergie**
16. *I Don't Need A Man* **The Pussycat Dolls**
17. *Sexy Love* **Ne-Yo**
18. *Me & U* **Cassie**
19. *It's Not That Easy* **Lemar**
20. *Unfaithful* **Rihanna**
21. *The Rose* **Westlife**
22. *Breaking Free* **Gabriella & Troy**

CD2

1. *America* **Razorlight**
2. *Chasing Cars* **Snow Patrol**
3. *Last Request* **Paolo Nutini**
4. *Nothing In My Way* **Keane**
5. *Never Be Lonely* **The Feeling**
6. *Empire* **Kasabian**
7. *When You Were Young* **The Killers**
8. *U + Ur Hand* **P!nk**
9. *LDN* **Lily Allen**
10. *Rock Steady* **All Saints**
11. *Coming Around Again* **Simon Webbe**
12. *Something About You* **Jamelia**
13. *Yeah Yeah* **Bodyrox feat. Luciana**
14. *Love Don't Let Me Go (Walking Away)* **David Guetta vs The Egg**
15. *Everytime We Touch* **Cascada**
16. *Borderline* **Michael Gray feat. Shelly Poole**
17. *Superfreak* **Beatfreakz**
18. *Chacarron* **El Chombo**
19. *Smiley Faces* **Gnarls Barkley**
20. *Star Girl* **McFly**
21. *Hey Kid* **Matt Willis**
22. *Jump In My Car* **David Hasselhoff**
23. *It's All Coming Back To Me Now* **Meat Loaf**

▶ Not content with twenty credited appearances thus far – the first of which was on this edition – Gallic groover **David Guetta** has lent his production skills to further *NOW* tracks by **Black Eyed Peas** ('I Gotta Feeling' on *NOW 74* and 'Rock That Body' on *NOW 76*), **Kelis** ('Acapella', also on *NOW 76*) and **Flo Rida** ('Club Can't Handle Me', *NOW 77*).

▶ Chelsea FC supporters hungry for more glory will be happy to hear that, thanks to **The Fratellis**, theirs is the only English top-flight football club whose name appears in the title of a *NOW* song.

NOW THAT'S WHAT I CALL MUSIC! '66

RELEASED 2 APRIL 2007

HELLO
LEONA LEWIS

GOODBYE
JAMELIA

▶ With a stuttering singles career most recently revived by head boy Samuel Preston's stint in the *Celebrity Big Brother* house, **The Ordinary Boys** signed off with their third of three appearances since *NOW 63*. However, Preston would go on to have continued success behind the scenes, writing 'Heart Skips A Beat' for **Olly Murs feat. Rizzle Kicks** (*NOW 80*), 'Beautiful' for **Enrique Iglesias and Kylie Minogue** and, perhaps most unusually, 'Dressed To Kill' for **Cher** in 2013, the title of which also became the name of her $55 million grossing 2014 tour of North America.

CD1

1. *Grace Kelly* MIKA
2. *Ruby* Kaiser Chiefs
3. *Walk This Way* Sugababes vs Girls Aloud
4. *Patience* Take That
5. *What Goes Around... Comes Around* Justin Timberlake
6. *Say It Right* Nelly Furtado
7. *Irreplaceable* Beyoncé
8. *Lil Star* Kelis feat. Cee Lo
9. *Smack That* Akon feat. Eminem
10. *Starz In Their Eyes* Just Jack
11. *Acceptable In The 80s* Calvin Harris
12. *Perfect (Exceeder)* Mason vs Princess Superstar
13. *Boogie 2Nite* Booty Luv
14. *Proper Education* Eric Prydz vs Floyd
15. *PATT (Party All The Time)* Sharam
16. *Truly Madly Deeply* Cascada
17. *I Think We're Alone Now* Girls Aloud
18. *Last Night A DJ Saved My Life* Seamus Haji feat. KayJay
19. *The Creeps* Camille Jones vs Fedde Le Grand
20. *Beware Of The Dog* Jamelia
21. *Wind It Up* Gwen Stefani
22. *Too Little Too Late* JoJo
23. *A Moment Like This* Leona Lewis

CD2

1. *How To Save A Life* The Fray
2. *Same Jeans* The View
3. *Standing In The Way Of Control* Gossip
4. *Catch You* Sophie Ellis-Bextor
5. *Golden Skans* Klaxons
6. *This Ain't A Scene, It's An Arms Race* Fall Out Boy
7. *Read My Mind* The Killers
8. *Window In The Skies* U2
9. *She's Madonna* Robbie Williams with the Pet Shop Boys
10. *Whistle For The Choir* The Fratellis
11. *I Luv U* The Ordinary Boys
12. *Open Your Eyes* Snow Patrol
13. *Before I Fall To Pieces* Razorlight
14. *She's My Man* Scissor Sisters
15. *Love It When You Call* The Feeling
16. *Sorry's Not Good Enough* McFly
17. *Alfie* Lily Allen
18. *Calm Down Dearest* Jamie T
19. *Easy* Sugababes
20. *You Know I'm No Good* Amy Winehouse
21. *I'm Gonna Be (500 Miles)* The Proclaimers feat. Brian Potter & Andy Pipkin

▶ Although not unique in plundering Rodgers and Hammerstein's *The Sound Of Music* (**JLS**'s 'The Club Is Alive' on *NOW 76* would also pay dubious homage), **Gwen Stefani**'s 'Wind It Up' – which incorporates an element of 'The Lonely Goatherd' – certainly had some of the more unusual credits of a *NOW* entry. Alongside the aforementioned Richard Rodgers and Oscar Hammerstein, songwriter **Pharrell Williams** rubbed shoulders with former **Haysi Fantayzee** front man and *NOW* star in his own right, Jeremy Healy (**Healy & Amos** *NOW 35*, **E-Zee Possee** *NOW 17*).

▶ Sharam Tayebi of **Deep Dish** (*NOW 59* and *61*) produced 'PATT (Party All The Time)' on *NOW 66*, essentially a remix of American actor and comedian Eddie Murphy's 1985 US No.2 hit single. Although Murphy does not have any credited UK Top 40 hits to his name, the soundtrack of his biggest and most recognizable box office hit – *Beverly Hills Cop* – has spanned three separate *NOW* entries of the title track, 'Axel F'. **Harold Faltermeyer**'s original could be found on *NOW 5*, **Clock** placed their cover version on *NOW 30* and **Crazy Frog** secured *NOW* canonization on volume *61*.

NOW THAT'S WHAT I CALL MUSIC! 67

RELEASED 23 JULY 2007

HELLO
MARK RONSON

GOODBYE
PAUL McCARTNEY

▶ 'Thnks Fr Th Mmrs' by **Fall Out Boy** is the only track in *NOW* history to not contain any vowels in its title. You could hear lead vocalist **Patrick Stump** twice on *NOW 67* – he also contributes to 'Cupid's Chokehold' by **Gym Class Heroes**, who appeared three times elsewhere in the series accompanied by **The-Dream**, **Adam Levine** and **Neon Hitch**.

TRACKLISTING NOW 67

CD1

1 *Umbrella* Rihanna feat. Jay-Z
2 *The Sweet Escape* Gwen Stefani feat. Akon
3 *Cupid's Chokehold/Breakfast In America* Gym Class Heroes
4 *Foundations* Kate Nash
5 *Girlfriend* Avril Lavigne
6 *Shine* Take That
7 *Do You Know? (The Ping Pong Song)* Enrique Iglesias
8 *Love Today* MIKA
9 *Real Girl* Mutya Buena
10 *Beautiful Liar* Beyoncé & Shakira
11 *Give It To Me* Timbaland feat. Justin Timberlake & Nelly Furtado
12 *Take Control* Amerie
13 *Candyman* Christina Aguilera
14 *Never Again* Kelly Clarkson
15 *Baby's Coming Back* McFly
16 *I Wanna Have Your Babies* Natasha Bedingfield
17 *Glamorous* Fergie feat. Ludacris
18 *LoveStoned/I Think She Knows* Justin Timberlake
19 *Because Of You* Ne-Yo
20 *I Wanna Love You* Akon Feat. Snoop Dogg
21 *Lost Without U* Robin Thicke

CD2

1 *Signal Fire* Snow Patrol
2 *Makes Me Wonder* Maroon 5
3 *Stop Me* Mark Ronson feat. Daniel Merriweather
4 *Here (In Your Arms)* Hellogoodbye
5 *Destination Calabria* Alex Gaudino feat. Crystal Waters
6 *Shine* Booty Luv
7 *The Girls* Calvin Harris
8 *Heavyweight Champion Of The World* Reverend and The Makers
9 *New Shoes* Paolo Nutini
10 *Dance Tonight* Paul McCartney
11 *Back To Black* Amy Winehouse
12 *Over My Head (Cable Car)* The Fray
13 *Either Way* The Twang
14 *Smokers Outside The Hospital Doors* Editors
15 *Your Love Alone Is Not Enough* Manic Street Preachers feat. Nina Persson
16 *Thnks Fr Th Mmrs* Fall Out Boy
17 *It's Not Over Yet* Klaxons
18 *Bigger Than Big* Super Mal feat. Luciana
19 *Get Down* Groove Armada feat. Stush and Red Rat
20 *What Am I Fighting For?* Unklejam
21 *Do It Again* The Chemical Brothers
22 *Sheila* Jamie T

▶ They've placed thirty-four singles in the UK Top 40 singles chart over the years, but 'Your Love Alone Is Not Enough' is, to date, the only *NOW* appearance for **Manic Street Preachers**. Helping them to make their debut here was **Nina Persson**, who has a stronger *NOW* pedigree, having been lead singer on all four inclusions by **The Cardigans**.

▶ It was a first *NOW* contribution for writer and producer to the stars Paul Epworth, with a co-write on **Kate Nash**'s single 'Foundations'. He has since helped pen 'Rabbit Heart (Raise It Up)' (*NOW 73*), 'Shake It Out' (*NOW 81*) and 'Spectrum' (*NOW 83*) for **Florence + The Machine**, **Plan B**'s 'Stay Too Long' (*NOW 75*) and 'Prayin'' (*NOW 77*), and 'Rolling In The Deep' (*NOW 78*) by **Adele**.

RELEASED 19 NOVEMBER 2007

**HELLO
NICOLE SCHERZINGER**

**GOODBYE
CRAIG DAVID**

OneRepublic's **Ryan Tedder** started his long and illustrious *NOW* relationship on this edition, having penned 'Do It Well' for **Jennifer Lopez**, as well as the **Leona Lewis** smash-hit 'Bleeding Love'. Tedder's own band would make their *NOW* debut on the next volume – with two separate tracks – and he would continue to contribute across the next twenty-one editions. 'Halo' by **Beyoncé**, 'Battlefield' by **Jordin Sparks** (both *NOW 73*) and 'Burn' by **Ellie Goulding** (*NOW 86*) are but three examples of his songwriting still to appear.

CD1

1 *Bleeding Love* Leona Lewis
2 *Rule The World* Take That
3 *2 Hearts* Kylie Minogue
4 *Valerie* Mark Ronson feat. Amy Winehouse
5 *About You Now* Sugababes
6 *Stronger* Kanye West
7 *Hot Stuff (Let's Dance)* Craig David
8 *Beautiful Girls* Sean Kingston
9 *No U Hang Up* Shayne Ward
10 *The Way I Are* Timbaland feat. Keri Hilson & D.O.E.
11 *Gimme More* Britney Spears
12 *Shut Up and Drive* Rihanna
13 *Sexy! No No No...* Girls Aloud
14 *With Every Heartbeat* Robyn And Kleerup
15 *Tired Of Being Sorry* Enrique Iglesias
16 *Song 4 Mutya (Out Of Control)* Groove Armada
17 *Like This Like That* Se:Sa feat. Sharon Phillips
18 *Let Me Think About It* Ida Corr vs Fedde Le Grand
19 *I Found U* Axwell feat. Max'C
20 *The Creeps (Get On The Dancefloor)* Freaks
21 *Waiting 4* Peter Gelderblom
22 *Love Is Gone* David Guetta and Chris Willis

CD2

1 *Hey There Delilah* Plain White T's
2 *1973* James Blunt
3 *Dream Catch Me* Newton Faulkner
4 *Worried About Ray* The Hoosiers
5 *She's So Lovely* Scouting For Girls
6 *1234* Feist
7 *In The Air Tonight* Phil Collins
8 *When You're Gone* Avril Lavigne
9 *The Heart Never Lies* McFly
10 *Mr Rock & Roll* Amy MacDonald
11 *Hold On* KT Tunstall
12 *Tranquilize* The Killers feat. Lou Reed
13 *It Means Nothing* Stereophonics
14 *Young Folks* Peter Bjorn And John feat. Victoria Bergsman
15 *Uninvited* Freemasons feat. Bailey Tzuke
16 *Big Girl (You Are Beautiful)* MIKA
17 *Tears Dry On Their Own* Amy Winehouse
18 *Do It Well* Jennifer Lopez
19 *Big Girls Don't Cry (Personal)* Fergie
20 *Don't Matter* Akon
21 *Baby Love* Nicole Scherzinger feat. will.i.am
22 *Home* Westlife

The **Freemasons** then. One half appeared as 'Small' with **Phats & Small** on *NOW 43*, and the Brighton DJs/producers would next appear (uncredited) remixing **Kelly Rowland**'s Top 5 hit 'Work' on *NOW 69*. 'Uninvited' on this volume was originally a US hit for notorious *NOW* conscientious objector, Alanis Morissette. 'Heartbreak (Make Me A Dancer)' on *NOW 73* would be the final appearance to date for both the **Freemasons** and, after a *NOW* career stretching back to *NOW 46*, **Sophie Ellis-Bextor**.

Sven Axel Hedfors (aka **Axwell**) is one third of progressive house superstars **Swedish House Mafia**, who would not make their *NOW* debut until volume *76* alongside **Pharrell Williams**. In the meantime, fellow Mafioso **Steve Angello** would get acquainted with *NOW* for the first time on *NOW 72*, while **Steve Angello** – in collaboration with **Axwell** – appeared as **Supermode** on *NOW 64* with their 'Smalltown Boy'-sampling 'Tell Me Why'. 'Smalltown Boy' by **Bronski Beat** originally appeared on *NOW 3*.

RELEASED 17 MARCH 2008

HELLO
ONEREPUBLIC

GOODBYE
NICKELBACK

▶ Joining modest entrepreneur **Kanye West** on 'Homecoming' was **Coldplay** front man **Chris Martin**, in a rare solo venture away from his regular band. **Coldplay** have to date placed fifteen tracks on *NOW*s – a feat which puts them joint top (with **McFly**) of the list of British bands made up of blokes with instruments.

CD1

1. *Mercy* Duffy
2. *Don't Stop The Music* Rihanna
3. *Now You're Gone* Basshunter feat. DJ Mental Theo's Bazzheadz
4. *Call The Shots* Girls Aloud
5. *Rockstar* Nickelback
6. *Stop And Stare* OneRepublic
7. *Sun Goes Down* David Jordan
8. *Work* Kelly Rowland
9. *Crank That* Soulja Boy Tell'em
10. *Piece Of Me* Britney Spears
11. *Heartbroken* T2 feat. Jodie Aysha
12. *What's It Gonna Be* H 'two' O feat. Platnum
13. *Come On Girl* Taio Cruz feat. Luciana
14. *Wow* Kylie Minogue
15. *Be Mine!* Robyn
16. *What Hurts The Most* Cascada
17. *Some Kinda Rush* Booty Luv
18. *Heater* Samim
19. *Just Fine* Mary J. Blige
20. *Ride It* Jay Sean
21. *Breathless* Shayne Ward
22. *When You Believe* Leon Jackson

CD2

1. *Chasing Pavements* Adele
2. *Apologize* Timbaland presents OneRepublic
3. *No One* Alicia Keys
4. *Happy Ending* MIKA
5. *Homecoming* Kanye West feat. Chris Martin
6. *Goodbye Mr A* The Hoosiers
7. *I Thought It Was Over* The Feeling
8. *Fascination* Alphabeat
9. *Elvis Ain't Dead* Scouting For Girls
10. *Just For Tonight* One Night Only
11. *Ready For The Floor* Hot Chip
12. *Flux* Bloc Party
13. *Something Good '08* Utah Saints
14. *The Journey Continues* Mark Brown feat. Sarah Cracknell
15. *This Is The Life* Amy MacDonald
16. *Pumpkin Soup* Kate Nash
17. *Change* Sugababes
18. *A&E* Goldfrapp
19. *Love Is A Losing Game* Amy Winehouse
20. *What A Wonderful World* Eva Cassidy & Katie Melua

▶ This was the first of eleven *NOW* appearances as a credited artist for **Taio Cruz**, a man who also boasts considerable success as a writer: he had won a Brit Award before his twentieth birthday for his role in 2005's British Single of the Year, 'Your Game', as recorded by **Will Young**. Elsewhere, his compositional skills have been evident on 'Take Me Back' (*NOW 72*) and 'Never Leave You' (*NOW 73*) for **Tinchy Stryder**, and **David Guetta feat. Usher**'s 'Without You' (*NOW 80*).

▶ 'Chasing Pavements' was our first *NOW* exposure to **Adele**, who would go on to sell thirty million copies of her second album, *21*, worldwide and appear on five *NOW*s thus far, including four consecutively from volumes *77* to *80*.

NOW THAT'S WHAT I CALL MUSIC! 70

RELEASED 21 JULY 2008

HELLO
DIZZEE RASCAL
GOODBYE
SCOOTER

▶ Originally published in 1929, 'Singin' In The Rain' is most famously associated with the 1952 Gene Kelly film of the same name. This **Mint Royale** cover version only reached No.20 upon its release here, but three years later topped the UK singles chart, having soundtracked the winning dance of *Britain's Got Talent* hoofer, George Sampson.

CD1

1. *American Boy* Estelle feat. Kanye West
2. *Dance Wiv Me* Dizzee Rascal feat. Calvin Harris & Chrome
3. *Singin' In The Rain* Mint Royale
4. *Black & Gold* Sam Sparro
5. *Warwick Avenue* Duffy
6. *Love Song* Sara Bareilles
7. *Sweet About Me* Gabriella Cilmi
8. *Closer* Ne-Yo
9. *Can't Speak French* Girls Aloud
10. *In My Arms* Kylie Minogue
11. *Denial* Sugababes
12. *SOS* Jonas Brothers
13. *10,000 Nights* Alphabeat
14. *That's Not My Name* The Ting Tings
15. *Always Where I Need To Be* The Kooks
16. *Propane Nightmares* Pendulum
17. *I'm Not Gonna Teach Your Boyfriend How To Dance With You* Black Kids
18. *Heartbeat* Scouting For Girls
19. *Turn It Up* The Feeling
20. *Cops And Robbers* The Hoosiers
21. *Have You Made Up Your Mind* Paul Weller
22. *Violet Hill* Coldplay

CD2

1. *Take A Bow* Rihanna
2. *No Air* Jordin Sparks with Chris Brown
3. *Heartbreaker* will.i.am feat. Cheryl Cole
4. *Love In This Club* Usher feat. Young Jeezy
5. *Touch My Body* Mariah Carey
6. *Better In Time* Leona Lewis
7. *With You* Chris Brown
8. *Stay With Me (Everybody's Free)* Ironik
9. *I Can Be* Taio Cruz
10. *We Cry* The Script
11. *Break The Ice* Britney Spears
12. *Scream* Timbaland feat. Keri Hilson & Nicole Scherzinger
13. *Low* Flo Rida feat. T-Pain
14. *Wearing My Rolex* Wiley
15. *You Wot!* DJ Q feat. MC Bonez
16. *All I Ever Wanted* Basshunter
17. *Jumping All Over The World* Scooter
18. *Discolights* Ultrabeat vs Darren Styles
19. *Watch Out* Alex Gaudino feat. Shena
20. *Cry For You* September
21. *Toca's Miracle* Fragma

▶ Although dance music's biggest global superstar **Calvin Harris** had previously appeared twice on *NOW* (debuting on *NOW 66*), 'Dance Wiv Me' with **Dizzee Rascal** on this edition marked the turning point in his career as the first of seven credited UK No. 1 singles in seven years. In addition to a jaw-dropping twenty *NOW* appearances across twenty-four volumes, Harris also holds the UK record for most Top 10 singles off one album – nine, from his 2012 release '18 Months'.

▶ And for their next trick, German trance overlords **Scooter** based their 'Jumping All Over The World' track on Sailor's 1975 No.2 hit 'A Glass of Champagne'. Sailor co-founder Phil Pickett would go on to greater award-winning songwriting success in the '80s as **Culture Club**'s unofficial fifth member, co-writing both 'Karma Chameleon' (*NOW 1*) and 'It's a Miracle' (*NOW 2*) with the band.

RELEASED 17 NOVEMBER 2008

**HELLO
THE SATURDAYS**

**GOODBYE
BOYZONE**

▶ The-Dream (born Terius Nash) had only this appearance with **Gym Class Heroes** as a credited *NOW* performer, but his impact on the series has been notable: as a writer or producer he had a hand in 'Umbrella' by Rihanna feat. Jay-Z (*NOW 67*), Mariah Carey's 'Touch My Body' (*NOW 70*) and 'Baby' by **Justin Bieber feat. Ludacris** (*NOW 76*).

CD1

1 *The Promise* Girls Aloud
2 *I Kissed A Girl* Katy Perry
3 *So What* P!nk
4 *Sex On Fire* Kings of Leon
5 *All Summer Long* Kid Rock
6 *Disturbia* Rihanna
7 *Miss Independent* Ne-Yo
8 *When I Grow Up* The Pussycat Dolls
9 *Beggin'* Madcon
10 *Forever* Chris Brown
11 *Spotlight* Jennifer Hudson
12 *You Make It Real* James Morrison
13 *Changes* Will Young
14 *Tattoo* Jordin Sparks
15 *The Winner's Song* Geraldine McQueen
16 *Girls* Sugababes
17 *Up* The Saturdays
18 *Love You Anyway* Boyzone
19 *Hot N Cold* Katy Perry
20 *Raindrops (Encore Une Fois)* Sash! feat. Stunt
21 *Angel In The Night* Basshunter
22 *Pjanoo* Eric Prydz
23 *Paddy's Revenge* Steve Mac

CD2

1 *Viva La Vida* Coldplay
2 *The Man Who Can't Be Moved* The Script
3 *Wire To Wire* Razorlight
4 *5 Years Time* Noah and the Whale
5 *In This City* Iglu & Hartly
6 *Shut Up And Let Me Go* The Ting Tings
7 *Never Miss A Beat* Kaiser Chiefs
8 *Take Back The City* Snow Patrol
9 *Love Is Noise* The Verve
10 *Infinity 2008* Guru Josh Project
11 *Dream On* Christian Falk feat. Robyn
12 *Stepping Stone* Duffy
13 *Handlebars* Flobots
14 *Spiralling* Keane
15 *Lies* McFly
16 *Boyfriend* Alphabeat
17 *Mountains* Biffy Clyro
18 *I Like You So Much Better When You're Naked* Ida Maria
19 *The World Should Revolve Around Me* Little Jackie
20 *Cookie Jar* Gym Class Heroes feat. The-Dream
21 *She's Like A Star* Taio Cruz
22 *Love Shy (Thinking About You)* Platnum

▶ The return of 'Encore Une Fois' for **Sash!** resulted in an eighth and final *NOW* appearance for the German production team. Sharing billing on this 2008 variation of the single was British outfit **Stunt**, who contained among their ranks one Molly Smitten-Downes – who would rise like a phoenix to seventeenth place in the 2014 *Eurovision Song Contest*.

▶ **Ronan Keating** has notched up twenty-eight *NOW* entries – either solo or with **Boyzone** – and, between 1995 and 2008, there was only one year where the ubiquitous Dubliner didn't turn out for a *NOW*. This edition marks the final appearance to date for **Boyzone**.

RELEASED 6 APRIL 2009

HELLO
LADY GAGA

GOODBYE
PET SHOP BOYS

▶ Upon release, **Alexandra Burke**'s 'Hallelujah' was the fastest-selling *X Factor* winner's single to date, selling just under 600,000 in its first week. 'Hallelujah', originally by Leonard Cohen, has appeared in various guises and scenarios since its original release in 1984, including the animated movie *Shrek* (2001), while Jeff Buckley's re-recording had featured on his 1994 debut, *Grace*. Although Cohen and Buckley re-charted the same week as Burke – with Buckley at No.2 behind the *X Factor* winner – neither of these artists have appeared on a *NOW* release.

178

CD1

1 *The Fear* Lily Allen
2 *Just Dance* Lady Gaga feat. Colby O'Donis
3 *Right Round* Flo Rida feat. Ke$ha
4 *The Boy Does Nothing* Alesha Dixon
5 *Just Can't Get Enough* The Saturdays
6 *My Life Would Suck Without You* Kelly Clarkson
7 *Take Me Back* Tinchy Stryder feat. Taio Cruz
8 *Day 'N' Nite* Kid Cudi vs Crookers
9 *Womanizer* Britney Spears
10 *Live Your Life* T.I. feat. Rihanna
11 *Right Now (Na Na Na)* Akon
12 *T-Shirt* Shontelle
13 *Mad* Ne-Yo
14 *Issues* The Saturdays
15 *Forgive Me* Leona Lewis
16 *The Loving Kind* Girls Aloud
17 *Can't Get Over* September
18 *Show Me Love* Steve Angello & Laidback Luke feat. Robin S
19 *Strong Again* N-Dubz
20 *Thinking Of You* Katy Perry
21 *Hallelujah* Alexandra Burke
22 *Hero* X Factor Finalists 2008

CD2

1 *Greatest Day* Take That
2 *Breathe Slow* Alesha Dixon
3 *Broken Strings* James Morrison feat. Nelly Furtado
4 *Love Story* Taylor Swift
5 *Sober* P!nk
6 *Human* The Killers
7 *Breakeven* The Script
8 *I'm Yours* Jason Mraz
9 *Don't Upset The Rhythm (Go Baby Go)* Noisettes
10 *Shake It* Metro Station
11 *Get On Your Boots* U2
12 *Kids* MGMT
13 *Omen* The Prodigy
14 *Let It Rock* Kevin Rudolf feat. Lil Wayne
15 *Cash In My Pocket* Wiley feat. Daniel Merriweather
16 *Heartless* Kanye West
17 *Dead And Gone* T.I. feat. Justin Timberlake
18 *Change* Daniel Merriweather feat. Wale
19 *Love etc.* Pet Shop Boys
20 *Rain On Your Parade* Duffy
21 *Islands In The Stream* Vanessa Jenkins, Bryn West and Sir Tom Jones feat. Robin Gibb

▶ Originally written by the Gibb brothers for Marvin Gaye, 'Islands In The Stream' was ultimately a global hit for Kenny Rogers & Dolly Parton twenty-six years before this tie-in with Comic Relief and popular BBC sitcom *Gavin And Stacey*. It is one of over ten **Bee Gees** cover versions to grace the *NOW* series, starting with 'To Love Somebody' by **Jimmy Somerville** on *NOW 18*, via 'Words' by **Boyzone** on *NOW 35* and two separate plunderings by **Steps** – 'Tragedy' on *NOW 44* and 'Chain Reaction', originally written for Diana Ross, on *NOW 50*.

▶ Last time around for **U2**: 'Get On Your Boots' was the nineteenth and to date final appearance for the Dublin globe-straddlers. Among groups, only **Girls Aloud** have more *NOW* entries.

RELEASED 20 JULY 2009

HELLO
EMELI SANDÉ

GOODBYE
THE PRODIGY

▶ Here began the *NOW* career of Armando Pérez – more commonly known as **Pitbull**. An unabashed collaborator, he has appeared twelve times on eleven *NOW*s over the years, yet only once on his own – here with 'I Know You Want Me (Calle Ocho)'.

TRACKLISTING NOW 73

CD1

1. *Poker Face* Lady Gaga
2. *Evacuate The Dancefloor* Cascada
3. *When Love Takes Over* David Guetta feat. Kelly Rowland
4. *I'm Not Alone* Calvin Harris
5. *In For The Kill* La Roux
6. *Number 1* Tinchy Stryder feat. N-Dubz
7. *Jai Ho! (You Are My Destiny)* A.R. Rahman & The Pussycat Dolls feat. Nicole Scherzinger
8. *Diamond Rings* Chipmunk feat. Emeli Sandé
9. *Not Fair* Lily Allen
10. *Mama Do (Uh Oh, Uh Oh)* Pixie Lott
11. *Please Don't Leave Me* P!nk
12. *Untouched* The Veronicas
13. *Waking Up In Vegas* Katy Perry
14. *Untouchable* Girls Aloud
15. *Release Me* Agnes
16. *Heartbreak (Make Me A Dancer)* Freemasons feat. Sophie Ellis-Bextor
17. *Let's Get Excited* Alesha Dixon
18. *Work* The Saturdays
19. *Up All Night* Take That
20. *If U Seek Amy* Britney Spears
21. *Battlefield* Jordin Sparks
22. *Stuck With Each Other* Shontelle feat. Akon

CD2

1. *Halo* Beyoncé
2. *Red* Daniel Merriweather
3. *Knock You Down* Keri Hilson feat. Kanye West and Ne-Yo
4. *Love Sex Magic* Ciara feat. Justin Timberlake
5. *Boom Boom Pow* The Black Eyed Peas
6. *Kiss Me Thru The Phone* Soulja Boy Tell'Em feat. Sammie
7. *Beautiful* Akon feat. Kardinal Offishall and Colby O'Donis
8. *Sugar* Flo Rida feat. Wynter
9. *Tiny Dancer (Hold Me Closer)* Ironik feat. Chipmunk and Elton John
10. *I Know You Want Me (Calle Ocho)* Pitbull
11. *Bonkers* Dizzee Rascal & Armand Van Helden
12. *Warrior's Dance* The Prodigy
13. *Don't Trust Me* 3OH!3
14. *Fire* Kasabian
15. *Rabbit Heart (Raise It Up)* Florence + The Machine
16. *Never Forget You* Noisettes
17. *New In Town* Little Boots
18. *Please Don't Stop The Rain* James Morrison
19. *Candy* Paolo Nutini
20. *We Are The People* Empire of the Sun
21. *I Remember* deadmau5 & Kaskade
22. *Poppiholla* Chicane

▶ 'Untouchable' was the twentieth and penultimate **Girls Aloud** single to feature on the *NOW* series, and was the first of their singles to miss the UK Top 10 – falling gallingly short at No.11. It immediately preceded the band's original split. A year later, a Facebook campaign to finally push the track into the upper echelons of the chart was not successful, as the revived single could reach only No.152.

▶ **Akon**'s double appearance here – as a featured artist with **Shontelle** on 'Stuck With Each Other' and joined by **Kardinal Offishal** and **Colby O'Donis** for 'Beautiful' – contributes to his lifetime *NOW* tally of thirteen. As male solo artists, only **Robbie Willams**, **Calvin Harris**, **David Guetta** and **Ne-Yo** exceed that score.

1
Entry for Whitney Houston
NOW 74

2
appearances from Kajagoogoo on the first volume

3
AM Eternal (Live At The SSL), The KLF
NOW 19

4
Appearances for Howard Jones across the first five volumes

5
Credited artists on one song. Has happened on 2 occasions*

6
Denim clad entries for Status Quo

Status Quo

7
Consecutive appearances for Cast

8
Appearances for Bananarama

Kelis

9
Entries for Kelis

10
appearances across first twenty *NOW*s for Jimmy Somerville

★'Thank Abba For The Music', *NOW 42* –
B*Witched, Billie, Cleopatra, Steps, Tina Cousins

'You Should Really Know', *NOW 59* –
Enya, Ishani, Naila Boss, Shola Ama, The Pirates

IT'S A SYNTH

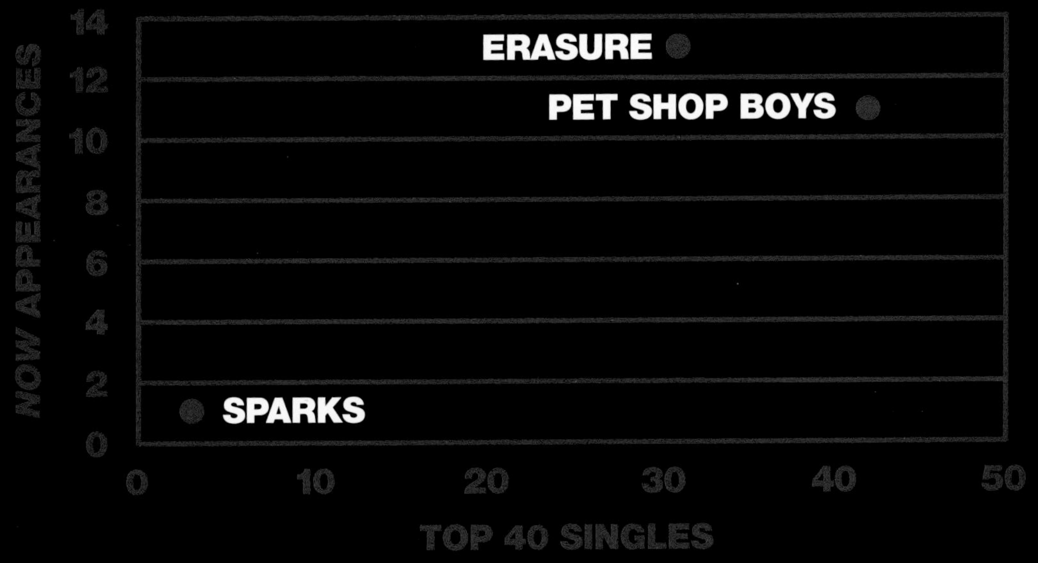

ERASURE
PET SHOP BOYS
SPARKS
NOW APPEARANCES
0
2
4
6
8
10
12
14
0
10
20
30
40
50
TOP 40 SINGLES

'THIS IS IT...THE PIG ONE!'

THOSE FAMOUS VOICES OF THE TV ADS

TRACEY ULLMAN
NOW 1

BRIAN GLOVER
NOW 3, 4 & 5

MARK GOODIER
***NOW 21* TO PRESENT**

RELEASED 23 NOVEMBER 2009

HELLO
JLS
GOODBYE
MIKA

▶ Anglo-Irish pop quintet **The Saturdays** steadily piled up thirteen *NOW* appearances in sixteen editions between *NOW*s *71* and *86*. Their philosophically unlikely inclusion here, 'Forever Is Over', was co-written by an unexpected combination of Sam Watters from *NOW 20*'s **Color Me Badd** and James Bourne of **Busted**.

CD1

1. *Fight For This Love* Cheryl Cole
2. *Haven't Met You Yet* Michael Bublé
3. *I Gotta Feeling* The Black Eyed Peas
4. *Sexy Chick* David Guetta feat. Akon
5. *Bulletproof* La Roux
6. *Break Your Heart* Taio Cruz
7. *I Need You* N-Dubz
8. *Whatcha Say* Jason Derülo
9. *Down* Jay Sean feat. Lil Wayne
10. *To Love Again* Alesha Dixon
11. *Oopsy Daisy* Chipmunk feat. Dayo Olatunji
12. *Never Leave You* Tinchy Stryder feat. Amelle
13. *Remedy* Little Boots
14. *Boys And Girls* Pixie Lott
15. *Left My Heart In Tokyo* Mini Viva
16. *Fire Burning* Sean Kingston
17. *Hotel Room Service* Pitbull feat. Nicole Scherzinger
18. *Get Sexy* Sugababes
19. *Forever Is Over* The Saturdays
20. *I Got Soul* Young Soul Rebels
21. *I Need You Now* Agnes
22. *Beat Again* JLS

CD2

1. *Paparazzi* Lady Gaga
2. *Sweet Dreams* Beyoncé
3. *She Wolf* Shakira
4. *Run This Town* Jay-Z feat. Rihanna and Kanye West
5. *Supernova* Mr Hudson feat. Kanye West
6. *Bodies* Robbie Williams
7. *Holiday* Dizzee Rascal
8. *Ready For The Weekend* Calvin Harris
9. *Million Dollar Bill* Whitney Houston
10. *Get Shaky* The Ian Carey Project
11. *End Credits* Chase & Status feat. Plan B
12. *Sweet Disposition* The Temper Trap
13. *Uprising* Muse
14. *Just Say Yes* Snow Patrol
15. *You've Got The Love* Florence + The Machine
16. *22* Lily Allen
17. *Pencil Full Of Lead* Paolo Nutini
18. *We Are Golden* MIKA
19. *Good Girls Go Bad* Cobra Starship feat. Leighton Meester
20. *Little Lion Man* Mumford & Sons
21. *The Day I Died* Just Jack
22. *Outta Here* Esmée Denters
23. *Ghosts 'n' Stuff* deadmau5 feat. Rob Swire

▶ Diverging fortunes for production power house Xenomania and their former charges on *NOW 74*. **Cheryl Cole** – formerly of Xenomania favourites **Girls Aloud** – delivered her first solo single on this edition, the million-selling 'Fight For This Love'. Elsewhere, the production outfit's new protégés – the highly tipped **Mini Viva** – delivered their sole Top 40 single, 'Left My Heart In Tokyo'. Twelve months later and it would be all over for the 'Viva. Harsh.

▶ Always the bridesmaid. In the UK, American rapper **Lil Wayne** has appeared four times across the *NOW* series but only ever in a supporting 'featuring' role. However, in the US the picture is somewhat different, with the artist also known as Dwayne Carter Jr enjoying one of the most successful musical careers of recent years. With over fifteen million album sales to his name, the illustriously inked Wayne also holds the record for most ever featured tracks on the *Billboard Hot 100* – 113 at time of writing.

RELEASED 22 MARCH 2010

HELLO
TINIE TEMPAH

GOODBYE
LEMAR

▶ Kilmarnock alternative rockers **Biffy Clyro** were involved in their second (of three) *NOW*s here with the powerful ballad 'Many Of Horror'. Three volumes later, the song would be back – retitled 'When We Collide' – in the hands of *X Factor* winner **Matt Cardle**, who took the song to the Christmas No.1 spot in 2010. **Biffy Clyro**'s original version re-entered the Top 10 in the wake of Cardle's recording.

CD1

1. *Bad Romance* Lady Gaga
2. *Starstrukk* 3OH!3 feat. Katy Perry
3. *Meet Me Halfway* The Black Eyed Peas
4. *Everybody In Love* JLS
5. *Replay* Iyaz
6. *Pass Out* Tinie Tempah
7. *TiK ToK* Ke$ha
8. *If We Ever Meet Again* Timbaland feat. Katy Perry
9. *In My Head* Jason Derülo
10. *Rude Boy* Rihanna
11. *Look For Me* Chipmunk feat. Talay Riley
12. *Don't Stop Believin'* Glee Cast
13. *On A Mission* Gabriella Cilmi
14. *Broken Heels* Alexandra Burke
15. *About A Girl* Sugababes
16. *Ego* The Saturdays
17. *Under Pressure (Ice Ice Baby)* Jedward feat. Vanilla Ice
18. *One Time* Justin Bieber
19. *Do You Remember* Jay Sean feat. Sean Paul & Lil Jon
20. *Cry Me Out* Pixie Lott
21. *The Climb* Joe McElderry
22. *Everybody Hurts* Helping Haiti

CD2

1. *Empire State Of Mind (Part II) Broken Down* Alicia Keys
2. *Fireflies* Owl City
3. *Young Forever* Jay-Z feat. Mr Hudson
4. *3 Words* Cheryl Cole feat. will.i.am
5. *You Know Me* Robbie Williams
6. *Don't Stop Believin'* Journey
7. *Dog Days Are Over* Florence + The Machine
8. *Hollywood* Marina & The Diamonds
9. *Starry Eyed* Ellie Goulding
10. *Many Of Horror* Biffy Clyro
11. *Stay Too Long* Plan B
12. *Never Be Your Woman* Naughty Boy presents Wiley feat. Emeli Sandé
13. *Won't Go Quietly* Example
14. *Riverside (Let's Go)* Sidney Samson feat. Wizard Sleeve
15. *Why Don't You* Gramophonedzie
16. *The Way Love Goes* Lemar
17. *Playing With Fire* N-Dubz feat. Mr Hudson
18. *Opposite Of Adults* Chiddy Bang
19. *BedRock* Young Money feat. Lloyd
20. *My Name* McLean
21. *Russian Roulette* Rihanna

▶ **Helping Haiti**'s charity rendition of **R.E.M.**'s 'Everybody Hurts' features vocals from *NOW* types **Leona Lewis, Rod Stewart, Mariah Carey, Cheryl Cole, Mika, Michael Bublé, Joe McElderry, Miley Cyrus, James Blunt, Gary Barlow, Mark Owen, Jon Bon Jovi, James Morrison, Alexandra Burke, Susan Boyle, JLS, Westlife, Kylie Minogue** and **Robbie Williams.** Including appearances made as members of bands, the above ensemble have 142 *NOW* tracks between them.

▶ Cheerio then to pop's favourite shape shifters, **Sugababes.** An impressive nineteen song return from twenty-three volumes; beaten only by **Girls Aloud** as Group With Most *NOW* Appearances.

RELEASED 19 JULY 2010

HELLO
SWEDISH HOUSE MAFIA

GOODBYE
PENDULUM

▶ The last of two appearances for 'You Got the Love' by **Florence + The Machine** (credited here as 'You Got The Dirtee Love' alongside **Dizzee Rascal**). The song has appeared an astonishing five times in total, with **The Source and Candi Staton**'s original version turning up on *NOW 19*, *36* and *63*.

CD1

1. *California Gurls* Katy Perry feat. Snoop Dogg
2. *I Like It* Enrique Iglesias feat. Pitbull
3. *The Club Is Alive* JLS
4. *OMG* Usher feat. will.i.am
5. *Gettin' Over You* David Guetta
6. *All The Lovers* Kylie Minogue
7. *Just Be Good To Green* Professor Green feat. Lily Allen
8. *Nothin' On You* B.o.B feat. Bruno Mars
9. *Alejandro* Lady Gaga
10. *Parachute* Cheryl Cole
11. *Te Amo* Rihanna
12. *Good Times* Roll Deep
13. *Commander* Kelly Rowland feat. David Guetta
14. *Dirtee Disco* Dizzee Rascal
15. *We No Speak Americano* Yolanda Be Cool & DCUP
16. *Hot* Inna
17. *Stereo Love* Edward Maya feat. Vika Jigulina
18. *Eenie Meenie* Sean Kingston and Justin Bieber
19. *Can't Be Tamed* Miley Cyrus
20. *Turn It Up* Pixie Lott
21. *Baby* Justin Bieber feat. Ludacris
22. *Solo* Iyaz
23. *Carry Out* Timbaland feat. Justin Timberlake

CD2

1. *She Said* Plan B
2. *This Ain't A Love Song* Scouting for Girls
3. *Wavin' Flag* K'NAAN
4. *Ridin' Solo* Jason Derülo
5. *Try Sleeping With A Broken Heart* Alicia Keys
6. *She's Always A Woman* Fyfe Dangerfield
7. *Hey, Soul Sister* Train
8. *Fire With Fire* Scissor Sisters
9. *Once* Diana Vickers
10. *Kickstarts* Example
11. *One (Your Name)* Swedish House Mafia feat. Pharrell
12. *Rock That Body* The Black Eyed Peas
13. *All Night Long* Alexandra Burke feat. Pitbull
14. *Candy* Aggro Santos feat. Kimberly Wyatt
15. *Dirty Picture* Taio Cruz feat. Ke$ha
16. *Until You Were Gone* Chipmunk feat. Esmee Denters
17. *Rescue Me* Skepta
18. *We Dance On* N-Dubz feat. Bodyrox
19. *Dancing On My Own* Robyn
20. *You Got The Dirtee Love* Florence + The Machine & Dizzee Rascal
21. *Acapella* Kelis
22. *Frisky* Tinie Tempah
23. *Watercolour* Pendulum

▶ As songwriter for hire with his backroom team The Smeezingtons, **Bruno Mars** had already landed a No.2 hit for **Sugababes** on *NOW 74* ('Get Sexy', incorporating elements from our old friends **Right Said Fred**'s 1991 hit, also a No.2), but he received his first performance credit with **B.o.B** on *NOW 76*. And what a start – the first of ten tracks across fourteen volumes and the first of five UK No.1 singles. Not to be outdone, **B.o.B** would also land a second No.1 single on the next volume of *NOW*, with 'Airplanes'.

▶ **Skepta**, who debuted here on *NOW 76*, is the brother of fellow grime artist **JME**. They appeared alongside each other on *NOW 83*'s 'Can You Hear Me (Ayayaya)'. **Skepta**'s real name is Joseph Junior Adenuga, whilst **JME**'s is… Jamie.

RELEASED 22 NOVEMBER 2010

HELLO
OLLY MURS
GOODBYE
JOE McELDERRY

▶ Tramar Dillard is more familiar to seasoned *NOW* watchers as **Flo Rida** and he too put in a double shift on this edition, accompanying **David Guetta** as he advised that the 'Club Can't Handle Me'. He also found time to contribute a rap to **The Saturdays** single 'Higher'. Of fourteen *NOW* tracks only three have been credited to Mr Rida on his own.

TRACKLISTING NOW 77

CD1

1. *Only Girl (In The World)* **Rihanna**
2. *Firework* **Katy Perry**
3. *Promise This* **Cheryl Cole**
4. *Club Can't Handle Me* **Flo Rida feat. David Guetta**
5. *Forget You* **Cee Lo Green**
6. *Dynamite* **Taio Cruz**
7. *Written In The Stars* **Tinie Tempah feat. Eric Turner**
8. *Cooler Than Me* **Mike Posner**
9. *Heartbeat* **Enrique Iglesias feat. Nicole Scherzinger**
10. *DJ Got Us Fallin' In Love* **Usher feat. Pitbull**
11. *All Time Low* **The Wanted**
12. *Please Don't Let Me Go* **Olly Murs**
13. *Pack Up* **Eliza Doolittle**
14. *Hollywood* **Michael Bublé**
15. *Get Outta My Way* **Kylie Minogue**
16. *Higher* **The Saturdays feat. Flo Rida**
17. *Green Light* **Roll Deep**
18. *Beautiful Monster* **Ne-Yo**
19. *Barbra Streisand* **Duck Sauce**
20. *Miami 2 Ibiza* **Swedish House Mafia vs Tinie Tempah**
21. *In My System* **Tinchy Stryder**
22. *My Wicked Heart* **Diana Vickers**

CD2

1. *Just The Way You Are* **Bruno Mars**
2. *Airplanes* **B.o.B feat. Hayley Williams of Paramore**
3. *For The First Time* **The Script**
4. *Shame* **Robbie Williams and Gary Barlow**
5. *Make You Feel My Love* **Adele**
6. *Slow* **Rumer**
7. *Impossible* **Shontelle**
8. *Just A Dream* **Nelly**
9. *Let The Sun Shine* **Labrinth**
10. *Billionaire* **Travie McCoy feat. Bruno Mars**
11. *Drummer Boy* **Alesha Dixon**
12. *Bang Bang Bang* **Mark Ronson & The Business Intl**
13. *Crossfire* **Brandon Flowers**
14. *The Cave* **Mumford & Sons**
15. *Prayin'* **Plan B**
16. *2012 (It Ain't The End)* **Jay Sean feat. Nicki Minaj**
17. *Best Behaviour* **N-Dubz**
18. *What If* **Jason Derülo**
19. *Broken Arrow* **Pixie Lott**
20. *Ambitions* **Joe McElderry**
21. *Party Girl* **McFly**
22. *Katy On A Mission* **Katy B**

▶ 'Pack Up' singer **Eliza Doolittle** is the granddaughter of noted educator Sylvia Young, whose theatre school bearing her name has seen many future *NOW* stars pass through its gates, including **Amy Winehouse, Billie Piper, Emma Bunton, Rita Ora, Javine, Matt Willis,** three quarters of **All Saints** and members of **The Saturdays, Little Mix, S Club 7, Union J, Five** and **McFly.**

▶ Upon its release, *NOW 77* was the highest-selling volume since 2003's *NOW 56*. With twelve No.1 singles included, it also established another record not beaten until *NOW 88*.

RELEASED 11 APRIL 2011

HELLO
JESSIE J
GOODBYE
AVRIL LAVIGNE

▶ 'Your Song' by **Ellie Goulding** was performed by the Herefordshire singer at the nuptials of Prince William and Kate Middleton in 2011, a poignant reminder of songwriter Sir **Elton John**'s own association with the royal family. The track also extends Elton's *NOW* career by another five volumes – his last artist credit was on *NOW 73*, but with 'Your Song' included here, he has a seventy-four volume reach that extends all the way back to *NOW 4* in 1984.

TRACKLISTING NOW 78

CD1

1. *Grenade* Bruno Mars
2. *Rolling In The Deep* Adele
3. *Do It Like A Dude* Jessie J
4. *S&M* Rihanna
5. *We R Who We R* Ke$ha
6. *Gold Forever* The Wanted
7. *When We Collide* Matt Cardle
8. *The Flood* Take That
9. *Your Song* Ellie Goulding
10. *Eyes Wide Shut* JLS feat. Tinie Tempah
11. *Who's That Chick?* David Guetta
12. *Higher* Taio Cruz feat. Travie McCoy
13. *Yeah 3X* Chris Brown
14. *Hold It Against Me* Britney Spears
15. *Happiness* Alexis Jordan
16. *Louder* Parade
17. *Thinking Of Me* Olly Murs
18. *What The Hell* Avril Lavigne
19. *Shine A Light* McFly feat. Taio Cruz
20. *L.I.F.E.G.O.E.S.O.N.* Noah and the Whale
21. *I Know Him So Well* Peter Kay and Comic Relief presents Susan Boyle and Geraldine McQueen

CD2

1. *Price Tag* Jessie J
2. *Champion* Chipmunk feat. Chris Brown
3. *Black And Yellow* Wiz Khalifa
4. *What's My Name?* Rihanna feat. Drake
5. *The Time (Dirty Bit)* The Black Eyed Peas
6. *Poison* Nicole Scherzinger
7. *Tonight (I'm Lovin' You)* Enrique Iglesias feat. Ludacris and DJ Frank E
8. *Bright Lights Bigger City* Cee Lo Green feat. Wiz Khalifa
8. *E.T.* Katy Perry feat. Kanye West
9. *F**kin' Perfect* P!nk
10. *Wonderman* Tinie Tempah
11. *Whip My Hair* Willow Smith
12. *Lights On* Katy B feat. Ms Dynamite
13. *Hello* Martin Solveig feat. Dragonette
14. *Who Dat Girl* Flo Rida feat. Akon
15. *Like A G6* Far East Movement feat. The Cataracs & Dev
16. *Traktor* Wretch 32 feat. L
17. *Like U Like* Aggro Santos feat. Kimberley Walsh
18. *Runaway* Devlin feat. Yasmin
19. *Let It Rain* Tinchy Stryder feat. Melanie Fiona
20. *Blind Faith* Chase & Status feat. Liam Bailey

▶ East London's melodious **Jessie J** opened her *NOW* account here with her first two hit singles 'Do It Like A Dude' and 'Price Tag'. She notched up ten appearances in short order between *NOWs 78* and *88*.

▶ **Peter Kay** returns on *NOW 78* as his female alter ego **Geraldine McQueen**. Duetting here with **Susan Boyle**, the 1984 musical *Chess* included the original 'I Know Him So Well' alongside a number of other previous **Abba** demos which were re-worked for the show. **Abba**'s own *NOW* career is a slim affair – they went on an indefinite hiatus before the first volume was released. A revived 'Dancing Queen' marked their only appearance, on *NOW 23*, although an all-star tribute was paid to the Swedes on *NOW 42*.

NOW THAT'S WHAT I CALL MUSIC! 79

RELEASED 25 JULY 2011

HELLO
DJ FRESH
GOODBYE
SCOUTING FOR GIRLS

▶ We said farewell – for now – to **The Black Eyed Peas** on *NOW 79*, as the band entered a hiatus they announced from the stage at a 2011 gig at Alton Towers. **will.i.am** was far from quiet and averaged one appearance per *NOW* from editions *81* to *88*. Peas singer **Fergie** has four *NOW* credits to her name away from the band.

CD1

1. *Someone Like You* Adele
2. *I Need A Dollar* Aloe Blacc
3. *The Lazy Song* Bruno Mars
4. *Don't Wanna Go Home* Jason Derülo
5. *Born This Way* Lady Gaga
6. *On The Floor* Jennifer Lopez
7. *Mr Saxobeat* Alexandra Stan
8. *Last Friday Night (T.G.I.F.)* Katy Perry
9. *Glad You Came* The Wanted
10. *Don't Hold Your Breath* Nicole Scherzinger
11. *Just Can't Get Enough* The Black Eyed Peas
12. *Love Love* Take That
13. *Nobody's Perfect* Jessie J
14. *Notorious* The Saturdays
15. *California King Bed* Rihanna
16. *Love How It Hurts* Scouting for Girls
17. *Every Teardrop Is A Waterfall* Coldplay
18. *I Want You (Hold On To Love)* Cee Lo Green
19. *Finish Line* Yasmin
20. *The A Team* Ed Sheeran
21. *Skinny Love* Birdy
22. *One Big Family* Templecloud

CD2

1. *Give Me Everything* Pitbull feat. Ne-Yo, Afrojack & Nayer
2. *Party Rock Anthem* LMFAO feat. Lauren Bennett & GoonRock
3. *Louder* DJ Fresh feat. Sian Evans
4. *Changed The Way You Kiss Me* Example
5. *Where Them Girls At* David Guetta feat. Nicki Minaj & Flo Rida
6. *Beautiful People* Chris Brown feat. Benny Benassi
7. *Bounce* Calvin Harris feat. Kelis
8. *How We Roll* Loick Essien feat. Tanya Lacey
9. *Super Bass* Nicki Minaj
10. *Spaceship* Tinchy Stryder feat. Dappy
11. *Unorthodox* Wretch 32 feat. Example
12. *Badman Riddim (Jump)* Vato Gonzalez feat. Foreign Beggars
13. *Sweat* Snoop Dogg vs David Guetta
14. *Save The World* Swedish House Mafia
15. *Bass Down Low* DEV feat. The Cataracs
16. *Buzzin'* Mann feat. 50 Cent
17. *Hitz* Chase & Status feat. Tinie Tempah
18. *Broken Record* Katy B
19. *Guilt* Nero
20. *What A Feeling* Alex Gaudino feat. Kelly Rowland
21. *Dirty Talk* Wynter Gordon
22. *Sun Is Up* Inna

It started here for **Ed Sheeran** and *NOW*: 'The A Team' was the eighth bestselling single in the UK in 2011 despite not topping the chart – it peaked at No. 3. Suffolk-schooled Sheeran has racked up nine *NOW* tracks in all thus far. As Ed worked his way up through the gig circuit he shared stages with Nizlopi ('JCB Song', *NOW 63*), **Passenger** ('Let Her Go', *NOW 85*), automobile pursuers **Snow Patrol** (seven appearances, *NOW 57* to *74*) and most recently reunion scotcher **Taylor Swift** (four showings from *NOW 72* to *85*).

▶ English hip hop and dubstep quartet **Foreign Beggars** are comprised of the following performers: Orifice Vulgatron, DJ Nonames, Dag Nabbit and Metropolis. Their collaboration with **Vato Gonzalez**, here on 'Badman Riddim (Jump)', was the only time they have graced the *NOW* archives.

NOW THAT'S WHAT I CALL MUSIC! 80

RELEASED 21 NOVEMBER 2011

**DOUBLE FEATURE
CALVIN HARRIS
RIHANNA
RIZZLE KICKS**

▶ After twelve years, twenty-four Top 10 singles, fourteen No.1s and six *NOW* entries, **Westlife** drew their record breaking career to a close with 'Lighthouse', a single co-written by **Gary Barlow**. It was their only single to that point to miss the UK Top 10. Like **Boyzone** before them, they were managed by *The X Factor*'s Louis Walsh, who between *NOW 30* and this edition of the series, would see either **Westlife**, **Boyzone** or a solo **Ronan Keating** feature on an incredible thirty-four separate occasions.

196

CD1

1 *Moves Like Jagger* Maroon 5 feat. Christina Aguilera
2 *We Found Love* Rihanna feat. Calvin Harris
3 *What Makes You Beautiful* One Direction
4 *Marry You* Bruno Mars
5 *Take A Chance On Me* JLS
6 *Jar Of Hearts* Christina Perri
7 *Mr Know It All* Kelly Clarkson
8 *Heart Skips A Beat* Olly Murs feat. Rizzle Kicks
9 *Lightning* The Wanted
10 *All About Tonight* Pixie Lott
11 *All Fired Up* The Saturdays
12 *The Edge Of Glory* Lady Gaga
13 *Jealousy* Will Young
14 *I Won't Let You Go* James Morrison
15 *You Need Me, I Don't Need You* Ed Sheeran
16 *Cannonball* Damien Rice
17 *Video Games* Lana Del Rey
18 *Wherever You Will Go* Charlene Soraia
19 *Iris* Goo Goo Dolls
20 *Run For Your Life* Matt Cardle
21 *Lighthouse* Westlife

CD2

1 *Set Fire To The Rain* Adele
2 *Read All About It* Professor Green feat. Emeli Sandé
3 *Stereo Hearts* Gym Class Heroes feat. Adam Levine
4 *Earthquake* Labrinth feat. Tinie Tempah
5 *It Girl* Jason Derülo
6 *No Regrets* Dappy
7 *Without You* David Guetta feat. Usher
8 *Feel So Close* Calvin Harris
9 *Collide* Leona Lewis feat. Avicii
10 *Stay Awake* Example
11 *Party All Night (Sleep All Day)* Sean Kingston
12 *Off The Record* Tinchy Stryder feat. Calvin Harris & BURNS
13 *Loca People* Sak Noel
14 *Down With The Trumpets* Rizzle Kicks
15 *With Ur Love* Cher Lloyd feat. Mike Posner
16 *Who's Laughing Now* Jessie J
17 *Cheers (Drink To That)* Rihanna
18 *Got 2 Luv U* Sean Paul feat. Alexis Jordan
19 *Heaven* Emeli Sandé
20 *I Need* Maverick Sabre
21 *Don't Go* Wretch 32 feat. Josh Kumra
22 *Teardrop* The Collective

▶ Another example of poacher-turned-gamekeeper on *NOW 80* was American singer-songwriter **Mike Posner** who returned with his second and final artist credit alongside **Cher Lloyd**. Having previously debuted on *NOW 77*, Posner would return behind the scenes co-writing 'Boyfriend' for **Justin Bieber** (*NOW 82*), 'Beneath Your Beautiful' with **Labrinth feat. Emeli Sandé** (*NOW 83*) and **Maroon 5**'s 'Sugar' (*NOW 90*). Conversely, this would be **Cher Lloyd**'s sole *NOW* appearance.

▶ And talking of the former Brit Award winner, **Emeli Sandé**'s imperial phased ubiquity started here. Despite two supporting credits to her name on *NOW 73* (**Chipmunk**) and *NOW 75* (**Naughty Boy** – their first of three *NOW* collaborations), her breakout hit 'Heaven' was featured on *NOW 80* alongside her collaboration with **Professor Green**, 'Read All About It'. Sandé would feature nine times between *NOW 80* and *NOW 90*.

RELEASED 2 APRIL 2012

HELLO
SIA

GOODBYE
JENNIFER LOPEZ

▶ **Little Mix** was the first group to emerge from *The X Factor* competition victorious and have amassed seven *NOW* appearances to date – the highest total for a winner of the show. Other *X Factor* winners in *NOW* history are **Leona Lewis** (five inclusions), **Alexandra Burke** (four), **Shayne Ward** (three), **Joe McElderry**, **Matt Cardle** and **James Arthur** (twice), and **Leon Jackson**, **Sam Bailey** and **Ben Haenow** (once). **Steve Brookstein** patiently awaits his opportunity.

TRACKLISTING NOW 81

CD1

1. *Somebody That I Used To Know* **Gotye feat. Kimbra**
2. *Paradise* Coldplay
3. *Lego House* Ed Sheeran
4. *Levels* Avicii
5. *Stronger (What Doesn't Kill You)* **Kelly Clarkson**
6. *Domino* Jessie J
7. *Titanium* David Guetta feat. Sia
8. *Good Feeling* Flo Rida
9. *Elephant* Alexandra Burke feat. **Erick Morillo**
10. *Last Time* Labrinth
11. *Mama Do The Hump* Rizzle Kicks
12. *Dance With Me Tonight* Olly Murs
13. *Get Yourself Back Home* Gym Class Heroes **feat. Neon Hitch**
14. *One Thing* One Direction
15. *Seven Nation Army* Marcus Collins
16. *Twilight* Cover Drive
17. *Alone Again* Alyssa Reid feat. **Jump Smokers**
18. *Who You Are* Jessie J
19. *Ray Charles* Chiddy Bang
20. *Proud* JLS
21. *Wherever You Are* Military Wives, **Gareth Malone & The London Metropolitan Orchestra**

CD2

1. *Sexy And I Know It* LMFAO
2. *Wild Ones* Flo Rida feat. Sia
3. *Marry The Night* Lady Gaga
4. *Next To Me* Emeli Sandé
5. *International Love* Pitbull feat. **Chris Brown**
6. *Dedication To My Ex (Miss That)* **Lloyd feat. André 3000 & Lil Wayne**
7. *She Doesn't Mind* Sean Paul
8. *Troublemaker* Taio Cruz
9. *The One That Got Away* Katy Perry
10. *Antidote* Swedish House Mafia vs **Knife Party**
11. *When I Was A Youngster* Rizzle Kicks
12. *Love Me* Stooshe feat. Travie McCoy
13. *Kiss The Stars* Pixie Lott
14. *You Da One* Rihanna
15. *Bright Lights (Good Life)* Tinchy Stryder **feat. Pixie Lott**
16. *Shake It Out* Florence + The Machine
17. *Take Care* Drake feat Rihanna
18. *Born To Die* Lana Del Rey
19. *Cannonball* Little Mix
20. *T.H.E. (The Hardest Ever)* will.i.am feat. **Mick Jagger and Jennifer Lopez**
21. *Rockstar* Dappy feat. Brian May

▶ Antipodean artist **Sia**'s voice was first heard on a *NOW* eleven years before her named debut here — she was the uncredited singer on **Zero 7**'s 'Destiny' on *NOW 49*. Making up for lost time, she placed two tracks on this *NOW* in collaboration with **David Guetta** and **Flo Rida**; her total currently stands at five.

▶ Who is the sprightly, preening gentleman making his *NOW* debut as a solo artist forty-nine years after his first chart hit? It's none other than rocking Knight of the Realm **Mick Jagger,** twenty-eight years after his first *NOW* appearance (**The Rolling Stones,** 'Undercover Of The Night', *NOW 2*).

RELEASED 23 JULY 2012

HELLO
RUDIMENTAL

GOODBYE
SCISSOR SISTERS

Easily done, but try not to confuse **D'banj**'s hip hop afrobeat hit 'Oliver Twist' with the Charles Dickens work of the same name. **D'banj** could clearly see the similarities, mind you, comparing the Dickens character's inability to secure the most meagre portion of starvation-abating gruel, with his own struggle to secure the love and attention of **Beyoncé**, **Rihanna**, **Nicki Minaj** et al.

200

TRACKLISTING NOW 82

CD1

1. *We Are Young* Fun feat. Janelle Monáe
2. *Call Me Maybe* Carly Rae Jepsen
3. *Payphone* Maroon 5 feat. Wiz Khalifa
4. *Whistle* Flo Rida
5. *Princess Of China* Coldplay & Rihanna
6. *Feel The Love* Rudimental feat. John Newman
7. *Starships* Nicki Minaj
8. *Where Have You Been* Rihanna
9. *R.I.P.* Rita Ora feat. Tinie Tempah
10. *Can't Say No* Conor Maynard
11. *Boyfriend* Justin Bieber
12. *Small Bump* Ed Sheeran
13. *Oliver Twist* D'Banj
14. *Black Heart* Stooshe
15. *Part Of Me* Katy Perry
16. *Primadonna* Marina & The Diamonds
17. *Picking Up The Pieces* Paloma Faith
18. *Drive By* Train
19. *Sparks* Cover Drive
20. *I Won't Give Up* Jason Mraz
21. *Too Close* Alex Clare
22. *My Kind Of Love* Emeli Sandé

CD2

1. *This Is Love* will.i.am feat. Eva Simons
2. *Call My Name* Cheryl Cole
3. *Hot Right Now* DJ Fresh feat. Rita Ora
4. *Young* Tulisa
5. *Turn Me On* David Guetta feat. Nicki Minaj
6. *Let's Go* Calvin Harris feat. Ne-Yo
7. *Scream* Usher
8. *Laserlight* Jessie J feat. David Guetta
9. *Turn Up The Music* Chris Brown
10. *Chasing The Sun* The Wanted
11. *30 Days* The Saturdays
12. *Euphoria* Loreen
13. *GreyHound* Swedish House Mafia
14. *212* Azealia Banks feat. Lazy Jay
15. *iLL Manors* Plan B
16. *So Good* B.o.B
17. *Level Up* Sway
18. *There She Goes* Taio Cruz
19. *Express Yourself* Labrinth
20. *Only The Horses* Scissor Sisters
21. *When She Was Mine* Lawson
22. *Sing* Gary Barlow & The Commonwealth Band

Daughter of Kosovar-Albanian parents, the multi-faceted **Rita Ora** makes her *NOW* debut on this edition with the first of eight appearances from the next ten albums – four of which reached No.1 in the UK singles chart. Alongside her musical career, Ora has also found time to act in the movies *50 Shades of Grey* and *Fast And Furious 6* as well as landing judging roles on both *The Voice* and *The X Factor*.

With **Soul II Soul**'s 'Back to Life' (*NOW 15*), **Sinead O'Connor**'s 'Nothing Compares 2 U' (*NOW 18*) and **Massive Attack**'s 'Protection' (*NOW 30*) to his name, legendary Brit producer Nellee Hooper returns to the *NOW* fold helming **Paloma Faith**'s *NOW* debut and first Top 10 single 'Picking Up The Pieces'. It was the first of four *NOW* entries to date for Faith – including a No.1 with **Sigma** on *NOW 89*.

32 YEARS, 18 CHRISTMAS NUMBER ONES

NOW THAT'S WHAT WE CALL FESTIVE

1986
Jackie Wilson
Reet Petite
NOW 9

1987
Pet Shop Boys
Always On
My Mind
NOW 11

1991
Queen
Bohemian
Rhapsody
NOW 21

1994
East 17
Stay Another
Day
NOW 30

1997
Spice Girls
Too Much
NOW 41

1998
Spice Girls
Goodbye
NOW 42

2000
Bob The
Builder
Can We Fix It
NOW 48

2001
Robbie
Williams &
Nicole Kidman
Somethin'
Stupid
NOW 51

2002
Girls Aloud
Sound Of The
Underground
NOW 54

2003
Michael
Andrews feat.
Gary Jules
Mad World
NOW 56

2005
Shayne Ward
That's My
Goal
NOW 63

2006
Leona Lewis
A Moment
Like This
NOW 66

2007
Leon Jackson
When You
Believe
NOW 69

2008
Alexandra
Burke
Hallelujah
NOW 72

2010
Matt Cardle
When We
Collide
NOW 78

2011
Military Wives
& Gareth Malone
Wherever
You Are
NOW 81

2013
Sam Bailey
Skyscraper
NOW 87

2014
Ben Haenow
Something
I Need
NOW 90

32 YEARS, 14 CHRISTMAS NUMBER TWOS

NOW THAT'S WHAT WE CALL FESTIVE

1986
The Housemartins
Caravan Of Love
NOW 9

1987
The Pogues & Kirsty MacColl
Fairytale Of New York
NOW 10

1991
Diana Ross
When You Tell Me That You Love Me
NOW 21

2002
One True Voice
Sacred Trust
NOW 54

2004
Ronan Keating & Yusuf Islam
Father and Son
NOW 60

2005
Nizlopi
JCB Song
NOW 63

2006
Take That
Patience
NOW 66

2007
Eva Cassidy & Katie Melua
What A Wonderful World
NOW 69

2009
Joe McElderry
The Climb
NOW 75

2010
Rihanna feat.Drake
Whats My Name
NOW 78

2011
Little Mix
Cannonball
NOW 81

2012
James Arthur
Impossible
NOW 84

2013
Pharrell Williams
Happy
NOW 87

2014
Mark Ronson & Bruno Mars
Uptown Funk
NOW 90

Shane MacGowan of The Pogues

NOW THAT'S WHAT I CALL MUSIC! 83

RELEASED 19 NOVEMBER 2012

HELLO
PSY

GOODBYE
MUMFORD & SONS

▶ They are, at the time of writing, true one-hit wonders – **Sam and the Womp** placed 'Bom Bom' at No.1 in the charts and have had no other success. However, bassist Aaron Horn's father Trevor has produced many a *NOW* tune since the very first volume when he worked the faders for **Malcolm McLaren** – most notably for **Frankie Goes To Hollywood, Seal, Paul McCartney** and **t.A.T.u.**

CD1

1. *Gangnam Style* Psy
2. *Candy* Robbie Williams
3. *Don't You Worry Child* Swedish House Mafia feat. John Martin
4. *We Are Never Ever Getting Back Together* Taylor Swift
5. *I Found You* The Wanted
6. *Sweet Nothing* Calvin Harris feat. Florence Welch
7. *One More Night* Maroon 5
8. *Can You Hear Me? (Ayayaya)* Wiley feat. Skepta, JME & Ms D
9. *I Cry* Flo Rida
10. *Let Me Love You (Until You Learn To Love Yourself)* Ne-Yo
11. *Good Time* Owl City feat. Carly Rae Jepsen
12. *Wide Awake* Katy Perry
13. *Blow Me (One Last Kiss)* P!nk
14. *Wings* Little Mix
15. *Waterfalls* Stooshe
16. *Hottest Girl In The World* JLS
17. *Pound The Alarm* Nicki Minaj
18. *Lost In Your Love* Redlight
19. *How We Do (Party)* Rita Ora
20. *Under The Sun* Cheryl
21. *Heatwave* Wiley feat. Ms D
22. *Bom Bom* Sam and the Womp

CD2

1. *Beneath Your Beautiful* Labrinth feat. Emeli Sandé
2. *Hall Of Fame* The Script feat. will.i.am
3. *Spectrum (Say My Name)* Florence + The Machine
4. *She Wolf (Falling to Pieces)* David Guetta feat. Sia
5. *We'll Be Coming Back* Calvin Harris feat. Example
6. *Anything Could Happen* Ellie Goulding
7. *Wonder* Naughty Boy feat. Emeli Sandé
8. *Turn Around* Conor Maynard feat. Ne-Yo
9. *Live While We're Young* One Direction
10. *Don't Wake Me Up* Chris Brown
11. *You Bring Me Joy* Amelia Lily
12. *Some Nights* Fun
13. *Say Nothing* Example
14. *Taking Over Me* Lawson
15. *Brokenhearted* Karmin
16. *Simply Amazing* Trey Songz
17. *Summer Paradise* Simple Plan feat. Sean Paul
18. *Wonderful* Angel
19. *Watchtower* Devlin feat. Ed Sheeran
20. *I Will Wait* Mumford & Sons
21. *One Day Like This* Elbow

▶ Watford all-rounder **Naughty Boy** appears four times as a performer but has played a writing or production role in three other *NOW* tracks: 'Diamond Rings' for **Chipmunk feat. Emeli Sandé** on *NOW 73* and Sandé's solo 'Heaven' and 'Clown' (*NOW 80* and *84*). The boy also played a part in **Sam Smith**'s rise to prominence by utilising his vocals on 'La La La' on *NOW 85*.

▶ With 'Candy', his first No.1 single for eight years, **Robbie Williams** returned to the *NOW* fold after a six edition absence and was placed second on the tracklisting for a fourth time. Only **Belinda Carlisle** has appeared in that position as often.

RELEASED 25 MARCH 2013

**HELLO
SAM SMITH**

**GOODBYE
GIRLS ALOUD**

▶ As with the Fugees' 1996 No.1 single of the same name, former Disney Channel actress **Bridgit Mendler** based the melody of her sole *NOW* entry 'Ready or Not' on the Delfonics' 1968 hit 'Ready Or Not Here I Come'. The track was originally produced by the legendary Thom Bell who, in 2003, enjoyed a return to the top of the UK singles chart having co-written and produced **Elton John**'s last solo UK No.1 to date, 'Are You Ready For Love' (*NOW 56*).

CD1

1. *One Way Or Another (Teenage Kicks)* One Direction
2. *Scream & Shout* will.i.am feat. Britney Spears
3. *I Knew You Were Trouble* Taylor Swift
4. *Just Give Me A Reason* P!nk feat. Nate Ruess
5. *Diamonds* Rihanna
6. *Pompeii* Bastille
7. *Impossible* James Arthur
8. *Troublemaker* Olly Murs feat. Flo Rida
9. *Locked Out Of Heaven* Bruno Mars
10. *Die Young* Ke$ha
11. *Ready Or Not* Bridgit Mendler
12. *DNA* Little Mix
13. *What About Us* The Saturdays feat. Sean Paul
14. *Something New* Girls Aloud
15. *Boomerang* Nicole Scherzinger
16. *Latch* Disclosure feat. Sam Smith
17. *Radioactive* Rita Ora
18. *Girl On Fire* Alicia Keys
19. *A Thousand Years* Christina Perri
20. *Clown* Emeli Sandé
21. *The Power Of Love* Gabrielle Aplin

CD2

1. *I Could Be The One* Avicii vs Nicky Romero
2. *Get Up (Rattle)* Bingo Players feat. Far East Movement
3. *Don't Stop The Party* Pitbull feat. TJR
4. *Drinking From The Bottle* Calvin Harris feat. Tinie Tempah
5. *Bassline Junkie* Dizzee Rascal
6. *Reload* Wiley feat. Chip
7. *Not Giving In* Rudimental feat. John Newman & Alex Clare
8. *Animal* Conor Maynard feat. Wiley
9. *White Noise* Disclosure feat. AlunaGeorge
10. *Rewind* Devlin feat. Diane Birch
11. *Standing In The Dark* Lawson
12. *Black Chandelier* Biffy Clyro
13. *My Songs Know What You Did In The Dark (Light Em Up)* Fall Out Boy
14. *Love Is Easy* McFly
15. *Only Love* Ben Howard
16. *Ho Hey* The Lumineers
17. *Little Things* One Direction
18. *Try* P!nk
19. *Please Don't Say You Love Me* Gabrielle Aplin
20. *Everywhere* Fleetwood Mac
21. *Explosions* Ellie Goulding
22. *He Ain't Heavy, He's My Brother* The Justice Collective

▶ There was a rare return to the Blondie back catalogue for **One Direction**'s *Comic Relief* cover version. The original was curiously never released as a single in the UK, however a previous *NOW*/ Blondie cover version – 'The Tide Is High' by **Atomic Kitten** on *NOW 53* – reached No.1 for both groups. The other half of **One Direction**'s medley – 'Teenage Kicks', originally by The Undertones – has never appeared on a *NOW* in its own right and neither have the band. Lead singer **Feargal Sharkey**, however, achieved *NOW* immortalization on both *NOW 4* and *6*.

▶ The power of 'The Power Of Love'. Across a twelve month period in the mid-80s, three separate songs charted with this same name. Huey Lewis reached No.9 whereas **Jennifer Rush** and **Frankie Goes To Hollywood** both reached the top spot. **Gabrielle Aplin**'s cover version, included here, also reached the summit. The original **Frankie Goes To Hollywood** version can also be found on *NOW 46*, while *another* completely unrelated 'Power Of Love' by **Celine Dion** is captured on *NOW 29*. Glad that's nice and clear.

RELEASED 22 JULY 2013

**DOUBLE FEATURE
PHARRELL WILLIAMS
DIZZEE RASCAL**

▶ **Gabz** – born Gabrielle Gardiner in Stevenage – was fourteen years old when she performed her original composition 'The One' on *Britain's Got Talent* in summer 2013 and when the renamed single 'Lighters (The One)' reached the Top 10 and *NOW 85*. She's not the youngest credited performer on a *NOW*, though – that honour goes to **Will Smith**'s daughter **Willow Smith** who was ten when 'Whip My Hair' appeared on *NOW 78*.

CD1

1. *Get Lucky* Daft Punk feat. Pharrell Williams
2. *Blurred Lines* Robin Thicke feat. Pharrell
3. *Let Her Go* Passenger
4. *Mirrors* Justin Timberlake
5. *La La La* Naughty Boy feat. Sam Smith
6. *I Love It* Icona Pop feat. Charli XCX
7. *Love Me Again* John Newman
8. *The Other Side* Jason Derülo
9. *True Love* P!nk feat. Lily Allen
10. *22* Taylor Swift
11. *Walks Like Rihanna* The Wanted
12. *Treasure* Bruno Mars
13. *Dear Darlin'* Olly Murs
14. *Heart Attack* Demi Lovato
15. *Come & Get It* Selena Gomez
16. *Let's Get Ready To Rhumble* PJ & Duncan
17. *Bounce* Iggy Azalea
18. *Antenna* Fuse ODG
19. *Hey Porsche* Nelly
20. *Still Into You* Paramore
21. *Radioactive* Imagine Dragons
22. *Lighters (The One)* Gabz

CD2

1. *Waiting All Night* Rudimental feat. Ella Eyre
2. *Wild* Jessie J feat. Big Sean & Dizzee Rascal
3. *Need U (100%)* Duke Dumont feat. A*M*E
4. *#thatPOWER* will.i.am feat. Justin Bieber
5. *Play Hard* David Guetta feat. Ne-Yo & Akon
6. *I Need Your Love* Calvin Harris feat. Ellie Goulding
7. *Feel This Moment* Pitbull feat. Christina Aguilera
8. *Reload* Sebastian Ingrosso feat. Tommy Trash & John Martin
9. *This Is What It Feels Like* Armin van Buuren feat. Trevor Guthrie
10. *Lost & Not Found* Chase & Status feat. Louis M^ttrs
11. *So Good To Me* Chris Malinchak
12. *You & Me* Disclosure feat. Eliza Doolittle
13. *Jack* Breach
14. *Lights On* Wiley feat. Angel & Tinchy Stryder
15. *Goin' Crazy* Dizzee Rascal feat. Robbie Williams
16. *Gentleman* Psy
17. *Chocolate* The 1975
18. *Carry You* Union J
19. *Gentleman* The Saturdays
20. *On My Way* Charlie Brown
21. *Another Love* Tom Odell
22. *It's A Beautiful Day* Michael Bublé

▶ Ladies and gentlemen, there were two songs with the title 'Gentleman' within three songs of each other towards the end of *NOW 85* – brought to us by Korean dance craze propagator **Psy** and long-running girl group **The Saturdays**. Only once before in *NOW* history had a title featured that word – **Wyclef Jean**'s 'Perfect Gentleman' on *NOW 50*. There's only 'Ladies Night' (**Atomic Kitten feat. Kool & The Gang**) in the vaults, although 'Lady' features six times across the years from 'The Lady In Red' (**Chris De Burgh**, *NOW 7*) to 'Treat Me Like A Lady' (**Zoe Birkett**, *NOW 54*).

▶ '22' has coincidentally been the title of two different *NOW* tunes, firstly on *NOW 74* by **Lily Allen** and again here, by **Taylor Swift.** No other number features as the sole constituent part of a song name more than once.

NOW THAT'S WHAT I CALL MUSIC! 86

RELEASED 18 NOVEMBER 2013

**DOUBLE FEATURE
AVICII
WILL.I.AM**

▶ 'Afterglow' by **Wilkinson** featured an uncredited vocal from **Becky Hill**, semi-finalist from the first series of *The Voice* in 2012. Becky would receive her first credited *NOW* entry two volumes later with 'Gecko (Overdrive)' alongside **Oliver Heldens**, a No.1 single. She was the first *The Voice* related act to top the UK singles chart. Leanne Mitchell, winner of series one, reached No.45 with debut single 'Run To You'.

CD1

1   *Roar* Katy Perry
2   *Counting Stars* OneRepublic
3   *Talk Dirty* Jason Derulo feat. 2 Chain
4   *We Can't Stop* Miley Cyrus
5   *Wake Me Up* Avicii
6   *Look Right Through* Storm Queen
7   *Animals* Martin Garrix
8   *Burn* Ellie Goulding
9   *Hold On, We're Going Home* Drake feat. Majid Jordan
10 *You're Nobody 'Til Somebody Loves You* James Arthur
11 *Do I Wanna Know?* Arctic Monkeys
12 *Royals* Lorde
13 *Youth* Foxes
14 *Applause* Lady Gaga
15 *Gorilla* Bruno Mars
16 *Best Song Ever* One Direction
17 *It's My Party* Jessie J
18 *Can We Dance* The Vamps
19 *Juliet* Lawson
20 *Show Me Love (America)* The Wanted
21 *Bonfire Heart* James Blunt
22 *Somewhere Only We Know* Lily Allen

CD2

1   *Eat Sleep Rave Repeat* Fatboy Slim and Riva Starr feat. Beardyman
2   *Thinking About You* Calvin Harris feat. Ayah Marar
3   *You Make Me* Avicii
4   *Earthquake* DJ Fresh vs Diplo feat. Dominique Young Unique
5   *Sonnentanz (Sun Don't Shine)* Klangkarussell feat. Will Heard
6   *Summertime Sadness* Lana Del Rey vs Cedric Gervais
7   *Bang Bang* will.i.am
8   *What I Might Do* Ben Pearce
9   *Count On Me* Chase and Status feat. Moko
10 *Children Of The Sun* Tinie Tempah feat. John Martin
11 *Other Side Of Love* Sean Paul
12 *R U Crazy* Conor Maynard
13 *Lifted* Naughty Boy feat. Emeli Sandé
14 *Lost Generation* Rizzle Kicks
15 *Boom Boom (Heartbeat)* Ray Foxx feat. Rachel K Collier
16 *Cheating* John Newman
17 *Big When I Was Little* Eliza Doolittle
18 *Disco Love* The Saturdays
19 *Afterglow* Wilkinson
20 *Booyah* Showtek feat. We Are Loud & Sonny Wilson
21 *Something Really Bad* Dizzee Rascal feat. will.i.am
22 *The Fox (What Does The Fox Say?)* Ylvis

▶ *NOW 86* featured the first solo appearance for Thomas Pentz, aka **Diplo**, alongside **DJ Fresh** (six NOW appearances to date) with his Top 3 hit 'Earthquake'. Pentz co-wrote Madonna's comeback single 'Living For Love': with seventy-one hit singles and zero appearances in the numbered series, Madonna remains *NOW*'s most infamous denialist. Alongside **Sia**, producer **Diplo** would co-write and produce the original version of 'Elastic Heart' for *The Hunger Games* soundtrack, before the Australian songwriter re-recorded a solo version of the track, which can be found on *NOW 90*.

▶ Tally ho! There was a distinctly vulpine flavour to *NOW 86* with both **Ray Foxx** and **Foxes** contributing and **Ylvis** viral sensation 'The Fox (What Does The Fox Say?)' adding to the skulk. Previously, we've also met **Samantha Fox** on *NOW 14* and, scampering into view just over the next hill, we find ourselves in hot pursuit of **Elyar Fox** on *NOW 87*.

RELEASED 7 APRIL 2014

DOUBLE FEATURE
LITTLE MIX

▶ Born Trevor Smith, **Busta Rhymes** has been having UK Top 40 hits since 1996 but first appeared on a *NOW* on edition *62*, featuring on and co-writing the **Pussycat Dolls** hit 'Don't Cha'. 'Thank You' on this *NOW* gathers hip hop veterans **Kanye West** (eleven appearances on *NOW*s), **Lil Wayne** (four features) and **Q-Tip** (who also appeared on *NOW 60*'s 'Galvanize' with **The Chemical Brothers**).

CD1

1 *Happy* Pharrell Williams
2 *My Love* Route 94 feat. Jess Glynne
3 *I'm A Freak* Enrique Iglesias feat. Pitbull
4 *Hey Brother* Avicii
5 *Dark Horse* Katy Perry feat. Juicy J
6 *Money On My Mind* Sam Smith
7 *Word Up!* Little Mix
8 *She Looks So Perfect* 5 Seconds of Summer
9 *Wrecking Ball* Miley Cyrus
10 *Nasty* Pixie Lott
11 *Story Of My Life* One Direction
12 *Let Me Go* Gary Barlow
13 *If I Lose Myself* OneRepublic & Alesso
14 *Ready For Your Love* Gorgon City feat. MNEK
15 *Wild Heart* The Vamps
16 *Do What U Want* Lady Gaga feat. R. Kelly
17 *Do It All Over Again* Elyar Fox
18 *Crying For No Reason* Katy B
19 *All Of Me* John Legend
20 *Say Something* A Great Big World & Christina Aguilera
21 *How Long Will I Love You* Ellie Goulding
22 *Skyscraper* Sam Bailey

CD2

1 *#SELFIE* The Chainsmokers
2 *Timber* Pitbull feat. Ke$ha
3 *Tsunami (Jump)* DVBBS & Borgeous feat. Tinie Tempah
4 *Under Control* Calvin Harris & Alesso feat. Hurts
5 *Wizard* Martin Garrix & Jay Hardway
6 *Red Lights* Tiësto
7 *I Got U* Duke Dumont feat. Jax Jones
8 *Of The Night* Bastille
9 *Kids Again* Example
10 *Move* Little Mix
11 *Braveheart* Neon Jungle
12 *Dibby Dibby Sound* DJ Fresh vs Jay Fay feat. Ms Dynamite
13 *Dr. Who!* Tujamo & Plastik Funk feat. Sneakbo
14 *Thank You* Busta Rhymes feat. Q-Tip, Kanye & Lil Wayne
15 *Million Pound Girl (Badder Than Bad)* Fuse ODG
16 *Out Of My Head* John Newman
17 *Turn Back Time* Sub Focus
18 *Control* Matrix & Futurebound feat. Max Marshall
19 *Let Go For Tonight* Foxes
20 *Can't Rely On You* Paloma Faith
21 *Dance With Me* Le Youth feat. Dominique Young Unique
22 *Hey Now* London Grammar
23 *Riptide* Vance Joy
24 *Best Day Of My Life* American Authors

▶ Co-writers of 'Dibby Dibby Sound' by **DJ Fresh vs Jay Fay feat. Ms Dynamite** here, backroom trio the Invisible Men also helmed **DJ Fresh**'s 'Hot Right Now' and other *NOW* hits for **Jessie J** ('Do It Like A Dude', 'Who's Laughing Now', 'LaserLight'), **Conor Maynard** ('Animal'), **Iggy Azalea** ('Fancy'), **Sugababes** ('Easy') and **Gabriella Cilmi** ('On A Mission'). Jason Pebworth and George Astasio of the Invisible Men were formerly the vocalist and guitarist for **Orson** (*NOW 63* and *64*).

▶ London quartet **Bastille**'s hushed 'Of The Night' was a mashup of two covers of previous *NOW* tracks: 'Rhythm Is A Dancer' by **Snap!** (*NOW 22*) and 'Rhythm Of The Night' by **Corona**, originally featured on *NOW 29*. The band won the Brit Award for British Breakthrough Act in 2014.

RELEASED 21 JULY 2014

**DOUBLE FEATURE
JESS GLYNNE**

▶ A truly global phenomenon, Academy Award winning 'Let It Go' by **Idina Menzel** from Disney's *Frozen* now ranks within the fifty biggest-selling singles of all time and one of the quickest to reach eleven million copies sold. In the UK, it is one of the best-selling tracks never to reach the Top 10.

CD1

1 *Ghost* Ella Henderson
2 *Sing* Ed Sheeran
3 *Stay With Me* Sam Smith
4 *Budapest* George Ezra
5 *Waves (Robin Schulz Radio Edit)* Mr Probz
6 *Problem* Ariana Grande feat. Iggy Azalea
7 *I Will Never Let You Down* Rita Ora
8 *A Sky Full Of Stars* Coldplay
9 *The Man* Aloe Blacc
10 *Love Never Felt So Good* Michael Jackson
11 *It's My Birthday* will.i.am feat. Cody Wise
12 *Fancy* Iggy Azalea feat. Charli XCX
13 *Loyal* Chris Brown feat. Lil Wayne & Tyga
14 *Extraordinary* Clean Bandit feat. Sharna Bass
15 *Right Here* Jess Glynne
16 *If I Go* Ella Eyre
17 *Classic* MKTO
18 *Don't Stop* 5 Seconds Of Summer
19 *Salute* Little Mix
20 *Me and My Broken Heart* Rixton
21 *Somebody To You* The Vamps feat. Demi Lovato
22 *Let It Go* Idina Menzel

CD2

1 *Rather Be* Clean Bandit feat. Jess Glynne
2 *Hideaway* Kiesza
3 *Gecko (Overdrive)* Oliver Heldens and Becky Hill
4 *Nobody To Love* Sigma
5 *Summer* Calvin Harris
6 *I Wanna Feel* SecondCity
7 *Jubel* Klingande
8 *Changes* Faul & Wad Ad vs Pnau
9 *Dangerous Love* Fuse ODG feat. Sean Paul
10 *Make U Bounce* DJ Fresh vs TC feat. Little Nikki
11 *Touch* Shift K3Y
12 *Always (Route 94 edit)* MK feat. Alana
13 *Wasted* Tiësto feat. Matthew Koma
14 *Anywhere For You* John Martin
15 *Take Me Home* Cash Cash feat. Bebe Rexha
16 *Don't Look Back* Matrix & Futurebound feat. Tanya Lacey
17 *Wiggle* Jason Derülo feat. Snoop Dogg
18 *Calling All Hearts* DJ Cassidy feat. Robin Thicke & Jessie J
19 *Welcome To The Jungle* Neon Jungle
20 *Chandelier* Sia
21 *Last Night* The Vamps
22 *Stay High (Habits Remix)* Tove Lo feat. Hippie Sabotage
23 *Only Love Can Hurt Like This* Paloma Faith

▶ The rise of **Jess Glynne** has been as meteoric as it has been swift – in eighteen months the Hampstead born singer and songwriter delivered six Top 10 singles, five of which appear over the next three volumes of *NOW*. Four were No. 1s. Her breakthrough collaborators **Clean Bandit** appear twice on this edition – once with Glynne on the multi-award winning 'Rather Be' and once with eighteen-year-old **Sharna Bass.**

▶ 'A Sky Full Of Stars' extends **Coldplay**'s *NOW* association to fifteen appearances since 'Yellow' on *NOW 46*, and in turn drops them into the Top 5 of the Most Featured Groups list (behind **Girls Aloud**, **Sugababes**, **U2** and **Boyzone**). The EDM-lite track was co-written with Tim Bergling – better known as **Avicii** – who is also of this parish (eight appearances between *NOW 80* and *NOW 91*). It was the band's fifteenth Top 10 hit in the UK.

NOW
THAT'S WHAT I CALL MUSIC!
89

RELEASED 21 NOVEMBER 2014

DOUBLE FEATURE
NICKI MINAJ

▶ **R. Kelly** has thirteen *NOW* appearances all told, stretching all the way back to volume *28* in 1994. The original version of 'Bump N' Grind' was on *NOW 30*, his third on the trot. The updated 2014 mix with **Waze & Odyssey** featured excerpts from a version of 'Push The Feeling On', also on *NOW 30* as recorded by the **Nightcrawlers**.

CD1

1. *All About That Bass* Meghan Trainor
2. *Wrapped Up* Olly Murs feat. Travie McCoy
3. *Bang Bang* Jessie J, Ariana Grande & Nicki Minaj
4. *Am I Wrong* Nico & Vinz
5. *Rude* Magic!
6. *I'm Not The Only One* Sam Smith
7. *Real Love* Tom Odell
8. *Wake Me Up* Gareth Malone's All Star Choir
9. *Don't* Ed Sheeran
10. *Blame It On Me* George Ezra
11. *Superheroes* The Script
12. *Love Runs Out* OneRepublic
13. *Maps* Maroon 5
14. *Take Me To Church* Hozier
15. *Boom Clap* Charli XCX
16. *Steal My Girl* One Direction
17. *Oh Cecilia (Breaking My Heart)* The Vamps feat. Shawn Mendes
18. *Amnesia* 5 Seconds of Summer
19. *Ugly Heart* G.R.L.
20. *This Is How We Do* Katy Perry
21. *Crazy Stupid Love* Cheryl Cole feat. Tinie Tempah
22. *Glow* Ella Henderson
23. *You Ruin Me* The Veronicas

CD2

1. *Blame* Calvin Harris feat. John Newman
2. *Changing* Sigma feat. Paloma Faith
3. *Prayer in C* Lilly Wood & Robin Schulz
4. *Real Love* Clean Bandit & Jess Glynne
5. *Don't Tell 'Em* Jeremih feat. YG
6. *Lovers On The Sun* David Guetta feat. Sam Martin
7. *Bump & Grind 2014* Waze & Odyssey vs R Kelly
8. *Break Free* Ariana Grande feat. Zedd
9. *Your Love* Nicole Scherzinger
10. *Fireball* Pitbull feat. John Ryan
11. *My Head Is A Jungle (MK Remix)* Wankelmut & Emma Louise
12. *Faded* ZHU
13. *Won't Look Back* Duke Dumont
14. *Wicked Games* Parra for Cuva feat. Anna Naklab
15. *T.I.N.A* Fuse ODG feat. Angel
16. *Walking With Elephants* Ten Walls
17. *Giant In My Heart* Kiesza
18. *Sunlight* The Magician feat. Years & Years
19. *Kisses For Breakfast* Melissa Steel feat. Popcaan
20. *Lullaby* Professor Green feat. Tori Kelly
21. *Black Widow* Iggy Azalea feat. Rita Ora
22. *Anaconda* Nicki Minaj

▶ A swift return to *NOW* for the song 'Wake Me Up', first featured on *NOW 86* by **Avicii** a short year before **Gareth Malone's All Star Choir**'s version. Recorded and promoted to benefit the 2014 *Children In Need* telethon, the choir contained no one with any previous *NOW* pedigree at all but did feature TV presenters John Craven and Mel Giedroyc, actresses Linda Robson and Alison Steadman and former footballer Fabrice Muamba.

▶ With twenty *NOW* appearances to date (and two remixes), fourteen of which have come between *NOW 80* and *90*, **Calvin Harris** now sits fifth in the all-time league table of most tracks featured. **Robbie Williams** sits at the top with twenty-nine, while **Rihanna** (twenty-five), **Kylie Minogue** (twenty-three) and **Girls Aloud** (twenty-one) are also ahead. Can Calvin claim the crown?

RELEASED 27 MARCH 2015

DOUBLE FEATURE

SAM SMITH
DAVID GUETTA
CALVIN HARRIS

▶ The golden boys of 2014/15 – **Sam Smith** and **Ed Sheeran** – continue their winning run on this edition, with Sheeran racking up his eighth appearance in three years and Smith, his sixth and seventh in little over one. Between them they have sold over eleven million albums across the world in the past twelve months.

TRACKLISTING NOW 90

CD1

1. *Uptown Funk* Mark Ronson feat. Bruno Mars
2. *Thinking Out Loud* Ed Sheeran
3. *King* Years & Years
4. *Sugar* Maroon 5
5. *Hold Back The River* James Bay
6. *Like I Can* Sam Smith
7. *Up* Olly Murs feat. Demi Lovato
8. *Lips Are Movin* Meghan Trainor
9. *Hold My Hand* Jess Glynne
10. *Elastic Heart* Sia
11. *Something I Need* Ben Haenow
12. *These Days* Take That
13. *Night Changes* One Direction
14. *Heroes (We Could Be)* Alesso feat. Tove Lo
15. *Heartbeat Song* Kelly Clarkson
16. *Pray To God* Calvin Harris feat. HAIM
17. *What I Did for Love* David Guetta feat. Emeli Sandé
18. *I Don't Mind* Usher feat. Juicy J
19. *When The Beat Drops Out* Marlon Roudette
20. *Ayo* Chris Brown & Tyga
21. *L.A. Love (La La)* Fergie
22. *So Freakin' Tight* Tough Love

CD2

1. *Wish You Were Mine* Philip George
2. *The Nights* Avicii
3. *Outside* Calvin Harris feat. Ellie Goulding
4. *Dangerous* David Guetta feat. Sam Martin
5. *GDFR* Flo Rida feat. Sage the Gemini & Lookas
6. *Gravity* DJ Fresh feat. Ella Eyre
7. *Higher* Sigma feat. Labrinth
8. *Promesses* Tchami feat. Kaleem Taylor
9. *I Loved You* Blonde feat. Melissa Steel
10. *Last All Night (Koala)* Oliver Heldens feat. K Stewart
11. *6 Words* Wretch 32
12. *Doing It* Charli XCX feat. Rita Ora
13. *Coming With You* Ne-Yo
14. *I Don't Care* Cheryl
15. *Say Something* Karen Harding
16. *Go All Night* Gorgon City feat. Jennifer Hudson
17. *Make Me Feel Better* Alex Adair
18. *Jealous* Labrinth
19. *Yours* Ella Henderson
20. *Wait On Me* Rixton
21. *Air Guitar* McBusted
22. *What Kind Of Man* Florence + The Machine
23. *Lay Me Down* Sam Smith

▶ **Busted**'s seven-strong consecutive run spans *NOW 53* to *59*, whilst **McFly**'s fifteen song relationship (including an unbroken innings between *NOW 58* and *68*) was still active as recently as *NOW 84*. Like a boy band *Avengers*, the two bands conjoined on *NOW 90* to produce the many headed, heartily inked pop hydra that is **McBusted** and scored their twenty-third entry for the family tree.

▶ And as we reach the *NOW 90* mark, it is a good time to reflect on the collective contribution of one of our most prolific pop gene pools: **Take That**. **Robbie** leads the pack with an unassailable twenty-nine entries, **Take That** themselves – bolstered by their first appearance here as a svelte trio – have chalked up twelve nods since *NOW 22*. **Gary Barlow** drops in with three solo entries to his name and, with barely time to take off his coat, **Mark Owen** pops by with a sole contribution on *NOW 56*. That's a colossal forty-five appearances in total or, quick maths, exactly 0.5 tracks per album.

NOW THAT'S WHAT I CALL MUSIC! 91

RELEASED 27 JULY 2015

DOUBLE FEATURE
KYGO
RUDIMENTAL
JEREMIH

▶ **LunchMoney Lewis** may have made his debut on *NOW 91* with hip hop poverty lament 'Bills' but he already had a family connection with the series – his father and uncle Ian and Roger Lewis were founder members of Jamiacan reggae outfit **Inner Circle**, whose 'Sweat (A La La La La Long)' featured on *NOW 25*.

TRACKLISTING NOW 91

CD1

1. *Love Me Like You Do* Ellie Goulding
2. *See You Again* Wiz Khalifa feat. Charlie Puth
3. *Cheerleader (Felix Jaehn Remix Radio Edit)* OMI
4. *Want To Want Me* Jason Derulo
5. *Black Magic* Little Mix
6. *Not Letting Go* Tinie Tempah feat. Jess Glynne
7. *Lean On* Major Lazer & DJ Snake feat. MØ
8. *Shine* Years & Years
9. *Get Stupid* Aston Merrygold
10. *Shut Up And Dance* Walk The Moon
11. *Poison* Rita Ora
12. *Somebody* Natalie La Rose feat. Jeremih
13. *Jealous* Nick Jonas
14. *Come And Get It* John Newman
15. *Bloodstream* Ed Sheeran & Rudimental
16. *I Really Like You* Carly Rae Jepsen
17. *Dear Future Husband* Meghan Trainor
18. *Trouble* Iggy Azalea feat. Jennifer Hudson
19. *Flashlight* Jessie J
20. *Let It Go* James Bay
21. *Ship to Wreck* Florence + The Machine
22. *Someone New* Hozier

CD2

1. *Are You With Me* Lost Frequencies
2. *Firestone* Kygo feat. Conrad Sewell
3. *House Every Weekend* David Zowie
4. *Hey Mama* David Guetta feat. Nicki Minaj, Bebe Rexha & Afrojack
5. *I Don't Like It I Love It* Flo Rida feat. Robin Thicke & Verdine White
6. *Runaway (U & I)* Galantis
7. *Where Are Ü Now* Skrillex & Diplo with Justin Bieber
8. *Freak Of The Week* Krept & Konan feat. Jeremih
9. *Worth It* Fifth Harmony feat. Kid Ink
10. *Five More Hours* Deorro x Chris Brown
11. *Bills* Lunchmoney Lewis
12. *Waiting For Love* Avicii
13. *Stronger* Clean Bandit
14. *Show Me Love (America)* Sam Feldt feat. Kimberley Anne
15. *All Cried Out* Blonde feat. Alex Newell
16. *Stole The Show* Kygo feat. Parson James
17. *Never Let You Go* Rudimental feat. Foy Vance
18. *Rumors* Pep & Rash
19. *Can't Stop Playing (Makes Me High)* Dr. Kucho! & Gregor Salto feat. Ane Brun
20. *Fester Skank* Lethal Bizzle feat. Diztortion
21. *Don't Look Down* Martin Garrix feat. Usher
22. *Talking Body* Tove Lo

▶ **Major Lazer** main man and LA-based DJ, rapper and producer **Diplo** appeared as a solo artist on *NOW 86*'s 'Earthquake' in tandem with **DJ Fresh** and **Dominique Young Unique**, and was the producer of **Alex Clare**'s 'Too Close' on *NOW 82*. Under his own name Diplo also appeared on *NOW 91* with **Skrillex** and **Justin Bieber**.

▶ **Jason Derulo**'s birth certificate has the surname Desrouleaux printed on it – the stage name Derulo is a spelling-friendly simplification. 'Want To Want Me' brought the Miami R&B merchant's *NOW* score up to a round ten, including four features running consecutively from his *NOW 74* debut.

Index

Page numbers in bold refer to *NOW* facts

B

Baby D, 79, 83, **113**
Babybird, 87
Babylon Zoo, 83
Backstreet Boys, **86**, 87, 89, 91, 93, 95, 107, 109, 111, 113, 117, 119, 123
Badly Drawn Boy, 127
Bailey Tzuke, 171
Baltimora, 17
Bamboo, 95
Bananarama, 11, 23, 27, 29, 31, **32**, 33, 39
Banderas, 51
Barbara Tucker, 97
Basement Jaxx, 107, 111, 119
Bass-o-Matic, 45
Basshunter, **117**, 173, 175, 177
Bastille, 207, **213**
Baz Luhrmann, 107
BBE, 87, 89
Beach Boys, 29, 83
Beardyman, 211
BeatFreakz, 161, 165
Beatmasters, **31**, 35
Beats International, **39**, 43
Beautiful South, **39**, 41, 45, 57, 67, 69, 81, 87, 89, 99, 101
Bebe Rexha, 215
Bebe Winans, 91
Becky Hill, **210**, 215
Bee Gees, **63**, 89, **179**
Beenie Man, **111**, 127, 129, 147
Belinda Carlisle, 31, 33, 45, 51, 53, 65, 85, 87, **205**
Bellefire, **119**
Bellini, 93
Beloved, **61**
Ben E King, 27
Ben Haenow, **198**, 219
Ben Howard, 207
Ben Pearce, 211

Benny Benassi, 195
Berlin, 27, **81**
Berri, 81
Betty Boo, 45, 59
Beverley Knight, **59**, 107, **123**, 149, 161
B*Witched, **98**, 101, **115**
Beyoncé, **65**, **90**, **119**, 129, 145, 165, 167, 169, **170**, 181, 185, **200**
B15 Project, 113
B-52s, 69
Bhangra Knights, 143
Biffy Clyro, 177, **186**, 187, 207
Big Ali, 165
Big Country, 9, 13, 23, 25
Big Fun, 41
Big Mountain, **69**
Big Sean, 209
Bill Medley & Jennifer Warnes, 51
Billie, 97, 99, 101
Billie Myers, 95
Billie Piper, 113, **115**, **117**, **191**
Billie Ray Martin, 79
Billy Bragg, 25
Billy Idol, **14**, 29, 31, **33**
Billy Ocean, **23**, 31
Billy Ray Cyrus, **59**
Bingo Players, 207
Birdy, 195
Biti, 67
Bitty McLean, 67, 69
Bizarre Inc, 59
Björk, **31**, 65, 67, 87
Bjorn Again, 59
Black Eyed Peas, **144**, 145, 147, 149, 151, 155, 157, 159, **161**, **165**, 181, 185, 187, 189, 193, **194**, 195
Black Kids, 175
Black Legend, 113
Blancmange, 11
Blink 182, 111, 119, 147
Bloc Party, 153, 173
Blockster, 101

Blonde, 219, 221
Bloodhound Gang, 113
Blow Monkeys, 27
Blue, **117**, **118**, 119, 121, 123, 127, 129, 145, 147, 149, 151, **159**
Blue Pearl, 45
Bluebells, 11, 61
Blueboy, 89
Bluetones, 85, **87**
Blur, **58**, 69, 71, 83, 85, 89, 101, **107**
B.o.B, **189**, 191, 201
Bob Marley, 11, 59, 109
Bob Sinclar, 157, 161, 165
Bob the Builder, **116**, 121
Bobby Brown, 39, 41, 73, 79
Bobby McFerrin, 35
Bobby Valentino, 155
Bodyrockers, 155
Bodyrox, 165, 189
Bomb the Bass, **31**, 35
Bombalurina, **37**, 45
Bon Jovi, 27, **85**, 115, 157, 161
Bonnie Tyler, 7, **40**, **72**
Boo Radleys, 73
Boogie Pimps, 147
Booty Luv, 167, 169, 173
Boris D'Lugosch, 119
Boris Gardiner, 25
Bowling For Soup, 127
Boy George, 27, **43**
Boy Wunda, 111
Boyz II Men, 93
Boyzone, **23**, 79, 83, 85, 87, 89, 91, 93, 95, 97, **98**, 99, 101, **107**, 111, **119**, **177**, **179**, **196**, **215**
Brainbug, 91
Bran Van 3000, 109
Brand New Heavies, 69, 71, 93
Brandon Flowers, 191
Breach, 209
Breathe, 35
Brian May, 55, 59, **129**
Brian McFadden, 153

S

First published in Great Britain by
Simon & Schuster UK Ltd, 2015
A CBS company

All *NOW*-related stats and miscellany by Pete Selby and Andy Healing.

1 3 5 7 9 10 8 6 4 2

Simon & Schuster UK Ltd
1st Floor
222 Gray's Inn Road
London WC1X 8HB

www.simonandschuster.co.uk

Simon & Schuster Australia, Sydney

Simon & Schuster India, New Delhi

A CIP catalogue record for this book is available from the British Library.

ISBN: 978-1-4711-5334-1

Design and layout by Nick Venables.
Cover design by Karl Heasman for The Design Corporation.

Photo Credits: p5 Featureflash/Shutterstock; p18 Landmarkmedia/Shutterstock; p21 James D. Morgan/REX Shutterstock;
p46 Nils Jorgensen/REX Shutterstock; p47 Roger Sargent/REX Shutterstock, Sheila Rock/REX Shutterstock; p48 Sunshine/REX Shutterstock;
p104 Helga Esteb/Shutterstock; p105 Brian Rasic/REX Shutterstock, JStone/Shutterstock; p162 Featureflash/Shutterstock;
p182 Yakub88/Shutterstock, Featureflash/Shutterstock; p183 Ilpo Musto/REX Shutterstock, Nils Jorgensen/REX Shutterstock, REX Shutterstock;
p203 Andy Soloman/REX Shutterstock;

Printed and bound in Italy by L.E.G.O. SpA.

Acknowledgements

The authors would like to thank:

Scott Macrae, Pete Duckworth, Steve Pritchard, Jenny Fisher,
Alex McCloy, Ashley Abram, Gary Debique, Mavis Sarfo,
Mark Addison and Pete Leggatt.

At Simon & Schuster: Nick Venables, Charlotte Coulthard,
Rumana Haider, Abigail Bergstrom, Suzanne King and Laura Hough.

Pete Selby would like to thank: Heavy Friends and Loving Family
but most especially Jo, Esmé & Finn.

Andy Healing would like to thank: Classical Rock Records,
Our Price, EUK and Sainsbury's. Dedicated to Lucy (in more
than one way), and to friends and family who continue to feign
interest when the fact cannon is deployed.